Perfect Praise Baby

P.O. Box 18008
Huntsville, AL 35804

Visit our web sites:
PrenatalMusic.net
EarlyChildhoodMusic.net
PerfectPraise.co

> This Material May Not Be
> Copied In Any Form…
> by Any Means
> Without The Expressed Written Permission
> of
> Perfect Praise, Inc.

Copyright 1999
2nd Edition- 2004
3rd Edition- 2008

ISBN-13: 978-1939747020
(Perfect Praise Publishing LLC)

ISBN-10: 1939747023

"Out of the mouth
of babes and unweaned infants
You have perfected praise."

Psalm 8:2, Matthew 21: 16
Paraphrase

Thoughts About
Perfect Praise Baby
From
Mrs. Denie Riggs

Early Childhood Music® is a preschool, piano-based music curriculum for children from prenatal to age seven years. Since 1998 we have witnessed many children enhanced by this God-centered, fun, piano-based program.

*This curriculum is taught in our own Early Childhood Music Schools in north Alabama. Since 2004, when we began tracking our Early Childhood Music® school graduates, **every** child who began by age five and graduated (usually around age 7 1/2) have three things in common.*

1. *They **all** are leaders in their schools, sports teams and churches.*
2. *They **all** excel in their academics. All of these children receive straight A's in school. Most are reading at three and four grade levels above their age.*
3. ***All** are amazing musicians with advanced ear training and musical skills. When they graduate from ECM they are able to play the piano in three major keys, two minor, transpose and compose their own songs. Most are under the age of eight years.*

Sound incredible? It is. But it is even more exciting when they start younger than age five. How can this be?

God has given Early Childhood Music® curriculum, the elements to be successful very early when windows of opportunity are open, during a child's formative years.

You are doing the best for your young child by creating an interactive musical environment. Singing, stomping, beating... and playing the piano changes how a preschool child's brain wires... and nothing enhances that development like music.

We bless you as you give your baby the best start... with Early Childhood Music®.

Mrs. Denie Riggs
Founding Director and Author
Early Childhood Music®~Give Them the Best Start

Perfect Praise Inc. is not responsible for injuries that occur due to an over-zealous caregiver who does not gently follow directions.

Do each activity carefully and gently.

Disclaimer

Neither Michael and Denie Riggs, nor Perfect Praise, Inc. or any of its associates or affiliates bear any responsibility for any health, life or disability issue with any child born who's parents have had access to or used any of the Perfect Praise, Inc. curriculum.

This disclaimer is not written to shed doubt on any of the principles included in this book. We firmly believe what we've written. However, we have no control over how this material is used by parents or care-givers who possess it.

Although music benefits are substantial, no guarantee is made as to *your* baby's progress or enhancement by using this curriculum or involvement in it's activities.

May God bless you and your family as you pursue this manuscript…

Michael and Denie Riggs

Table of Contents

	Page Number	Song on CD
Our Perfect Praise Baby Curriculum	10	
Our Perfect Praise Baby CD	11	
Your Perfect Praise Baby and Music Research!	12	
Music's Origin	12	
Music's Power	14	
Music Biblically Defined	14	
Music Affects Our Body	16	
Music Benefits Our Souls	19	
Music Benefits Our Spirit	22	
Right Brain, Left Brain or One Mind?	23	
Early Training	24	
Let's Recap...	28	
Spiritually Impart To Your Perfect Praise Baby	29	
Sing to Your Perfect Praise Baby	31	
What to Sing	32	
Create Soothing Surrounding Sounds For Your Perfect Praise Baby	33	
Baby-Approved (Preferred) Classical Styles	33	
Preferred Music, When and Where	35	
Praise and Worship Music	37	
Perfect Praise's Classical Praise CD	38	
Bounce Your Perfect Praise Baby	39	
Read to Your Perfect Praise Baby	40	
Creating Musical Experiences For Your Perfect Praise Baby	41	
Developmental Stages of Your Perfect Praise Baby	45	
Table of Contents continued ...		

Table of Contents

	Page Number	Song on CD
Lullabies and Rocking Songs for Your Perfect Praise Baby	46	
Hush Little Baby	47	1
God is So Good	47	2
Snuggle Up With Me	48	3
Kum Ba Ya	49	4
The Rocking Song	49	5
Lullaby Time	50	6
Alleluia	50	7
God is Love	50	8
From the Womb	51	9
Butterflies Flap Their Wings	51	10
Jesus Loves Me	52	11
Jesus Loves the Little Children	53	12
Massage Rhymes For Your Perfect Praise Baby	54	
Little Hot Dog	55	
Fresh As the Dew	56	
One Leg, Two Leg	57	
Wash the Dishes	58	
Round and Round the Garden	59	
A Little Flea Went Walking	60	
Two Little Eyes	61	
Criss-Cross Applesauce	62	
Round and Round the Haystack	63	
Little Angel Mine	64	
Diaper Games For Your Perfect Praise Baby	65	
Going On A Bike Ride	66	13
Table of Contents continued ...		

Table of Contents

	Page Number	Song on CD
Shoe A Little Horse	67	
Roly-Poly, Roly-Poly	68	
Peek-A-Boo!	69	14
Peek-A-Boo! I See You!	70	15
Gray Squirrel	71	16
Our Prayers Touched Heaven	72	
There's a Cobbler	73	
Kick Your Little Foot	74	17
Wiggles For Your Perfect Praise Baby	75	
Baby's Finger Play	75	
Toe Play Chant	75	
Open Shut Them	76	18
Pat-a-Cake, Pat-a-Cake	77	
The Little Mice	78	19
Five Little Kittens	79	
The Little Piggy Went to Market	80	
Whoops Johnny	81	
This Little Cow Eats Grass	82	
The Family Chant	83	
Floor and Chair Games for Your Perfect Praise Baby	84	
The Jack-in-the-Box	85	20
Little Fire Fighters	86	
Our Darling Little Baby	87	
Humpty Dumpty	88	
Two Little Apples	89	21
Jack & Jill	90	22
Table of Contents continued ...		

Table of Contents

	Page Number	Song on CD
Bouncing Games For Your Perfect Praise Baby	91	
Walter, Walter Wag Tail	92	23
Ride a Little Horsy	93	
The Horse Chant	94	
Riding On A Pony	95	24
I Know a Little Pony	96	25
Mother and Father and Uncle John	97	
See the Pony Galloping	98	26
I'm Riding My Horse	99	27
Instrumental Games For Your Perfect Praise Baby	100	
Everybody Praise the Lord	101	28
Twinkle, Twinkle Little Star	101	29
It's Music Time	101	30
This Little Light of Mine	102	31
Wheels on the Bus	102	32
Tick Tock	103	33
Hickory, Dickory Dock	103	34
If You're Happy and You Know It	104	35
Xylophone Songs For Your Perfect Praise Baby	105	
***Solfege* and Xylophone Stimulation Exercises**	105	
I Know	106	
The Flea	107	
Table of Contents continued ...		

Table of Contents

	Page Number	*Song on CD*
Circle Dances For Your Perfect Praise Baby	108	
Basic Carrying Positions	108	
Folk Dance Steps	109	
Bingo	109	36
Make a Joyful Noise	110	37
Clap Your Hands	111	38
Hoop Song	112	39
Looby Loo	113	40
Hokey Pokey	114	41
Crab Walk	115	42
Hello/Goodbye Song	116	43
Perfect Praise Baby Resources	117	
Our Perfect Praise Baby Success Stories	121	
Our *Give Them the Best Start* Prenatal Curriculum	122	
Contact Information	123	

Our
Perfect Praise Baby
Curriculum

In our *Perfect Praise Baby* curriculum contains:

1. The benefits of music for your baby's development. We explain why and how to use this incredible research to enhance your baby.

2. A few case studies of babies just like yours, who have used our *Early Childhood Music*® music.

3. Your tools of impartation. These include: singing to your baby; reading to your baby, surrounding your baby with soothing sounds; what to listen to and when, the power of bouncing your baby and much more.

4. Forty-three songs with lyrics on split-track CD.

5. Twenty-nine rhythmic chants and massage rhymes.

6. Xylophone songs.

7. Twenty-one ideas for incorporating all styles of music into your baby's world.

8. How to use this book's activities for the different developmental stages of your baby to age eighteen months and beyond.

9. Musical activities divided into sections: *Lullaby and Rocking Songs, Massage Rhymes, Diaper Games, Wiggles, Floor and Chair Games, Bouncing Games, Instrumental Games, Xylophone Songs and Circle Dances.*

10. Over 200 variations, ideas and positions to use for various developmental stages. Each variation is indicated by ♫.

11. Opportunity to purchase a rhythm instrument pack and precision-tuned xylophone through *Perfect Praise, Inc.*

Our
Perfect Praise Baby
CD

Our *Perfect Praise Baby* CD is in split-track format. If you play your CD in a stereo system, the balance control will change the balance between the background and the vocals.

♪ To listen to both background and singing voices, set the balance in the center for equal balance.

♪ To listen to the background only, set the balance for left only.

♪ To listen to the singing voice only, set the balance for right only.

Remember it is <u>your</u> voice that your baby responds to so after you have learned the songs, we encourage you to set your player for just the musical background and sing <u>alone</u> to your baby.

But the important thing is that you listen to your CD daily and sing along.

Your
Perfect Praise Baby
And
Music Research!

Before we get into the heart of this book, we want to give you some music benefit research to help you see the magnitude of that you are stepping into for your child.

This section of your book will cover these topics:
- Music: Its Origin and Power
- Music Biblically Defined
- Music Benefits for Spirit, Soul and Body
- Right Brain, Left Brain or One Mind?

Let's get started!

Music's Origin

What is music? When and where did it come from?

I must admit that I have been a musician since age three, played piano for church since age ten, taught piano since age twelve and was a music major in college but I never took time to define *music* or checked into its origin. Thus, even as a musician, I spent most of my life to this point unaware of the power and potential that music contains.

Music from Webster's dictionary is defined as, *"the art of the muses, the art of combining tones to form expressive compositions ...*[1]*"*

"The art of the muses..." Muses? Muses and musing are not words common in our modern world. Webster defines "muse" as *"to think deeply, to meditate."*[2]

So *music* may be defined as the *art of deep expressive meditation with tones.*

Where did music come from?

<u>God</u> created it. God knew that it would be important ... so He created it *first*!

Now, you may say, wait a minute ... I don't remember it that way!

Let's look at it in Genesis 1:3, "And God said, Let there be light; and there was light."

What did God create first? LIGHT!

Modern scientists tell us that light/music/sound are just different frequencies of the same spectrum. When God spoke LIGHT into existence, MUSIC was created!

God created music/light/sound <u>first</u>!

Everything in our universe is orderly *and* musical ... from the waves of the ocean to the cycles of the moon. **Bodes Law** says that each planet gives off its own musical tone ... exactly one octave apart from another planet. These sounds are so low that they are inaudible to the human ear, but they exist nonetheless. Scientists tell us that this **musical order** is the only thing that keeps the planets from crashing into one another.[3]

So if you put our definition of music with this scientific knowledge, the planets are expressively meditating with tones; i.e. making music.

The rainbow is also orderly and musical. Scientists tell us that if you could see middle C twelve or twenty-four octaves higher than you can hear, you would see color.[4] So when we see the rainbow, we witness the order of God's musical creation. Remember that the rainbow is the symbol of God's covenant with us. His symbol never changes and each color represents the notes of the musical scale. It's a musical symbol and it is *awesome*!

But it gets even better!

You've heard of DNA ... the newest crime fighting break through in our modern world. Each person has DNA that is individual to them ... as individual as their fingerprint. If you were to talk to a scientist regarding DNA, he/she would tell you when your DNA is decoded ... it is a song, *music*.[5]

God has created each of us to <u>be</u> a song! Your song is different than your husband's song. This gives new insight into dwelling in "harmony" with your spouse and those around you.

> *As musical beings, in a musical world, nothing touches us like <u>music</u>.*

We would venture to say that aside from Jesus, God's Word, our relationship with Him and prayer, <u>music</u> is the greatest gift that God has given us to bring confidence and peace into a troubled world, to enhance our development and to restore our spirit. And brings enhancement to every member of your family, especially your baby.

Music's Power

Think for a moment about the power of *light* … the laser light … the lightening bolt! Light transforms everything about us. There is just one thing that can cut through three feet of steel. *LIGHT!*

Light, music and sound are different frequencies of the same spectrum. *So the power of light is the power of music.*

With this in mind, think of the amazing benefits that you are pouring into your developing baby by your taking time to create a musical environment for him/her.

You will see that power in the pages ahead.

But before we move on, however, let's look deeper into the definition of music from God's Word. (This is like digging for gold … it's worth your time!)

Music Biblically Defined

The word *musician* only occurs once in the New Testament. (Rev. 18:22) It is the Greek word "mousikos" and is translated also "minstrel." It refers to one who is "musical."

It comes from a root word which is *'one who muses'*. Remember that Webster defined music as *the art of the muses*. A study of the word "musing" in its only occurrence in the Bible (Psalm 39:3) shows us that it is directly translated "meditation." The Hebrew word, "hagiyg," is akin to the root word "hagah" which means *to ponder, imagine, meditate and study*.

Here's the picture from Webster (man) and the Bible (God): to participate in making music is to also participate in <u>musing</u>, which is *to ponder, imagine, meditate and study*. And if that were not enough proof of the mental power of music and of music's underlying automatic cause and effect, here's more …

The Hebrew and specifically King David's musicians were so aware of the meditative power of music that they had a musical term and notation for it. It is the "higgayown". This word is probably similar to our modern term *affettuoso*, which is a musical term that indicates it is time to meditate on that specific part of the music.

This is all related to occurrences of the word *meditate* or *meditation* in Psalm 19:14, for example. Literally it is our thoughts ascending to God as sweet fragrance from an acceptable sacrifice.

Meditation of the thoughts and Word of God, day and night, produces success and prosperity in *everything* we do. (Joshua 1:9, Psalm 1:1-3)

The right kind of music *will* yield this in our lives, *because* music is meditation.

> Music produces brain function which causes incredible, active thought.

Now, this study was really deep, and you may have to ponder on it for a few days. That's okay. Keep reading and soon you'll see that what you are stepping into for your baby, is more than just a few singing songs.

Music Affects Our Body

The physical benefits of music are astounding for all ages, but especially for a prenatal baby and a very young child who's body and brain are forming.

The auditory nerve connects the inner ear with *the autonomic nervous system,* the part that regulates our body without our having to think about them … the heart, the lungs, the liver, etc.

As you read about these benefits, remember that by surrounding your baby's environment with music, all of these benefits are pouring into every developing cell, enhancing them for life.

Don Campbell's book, *The Mozart Effect*,[6] was one of the first books to teach the benefits of listening to classical music. Mr. Campbell's book studied Mozart in particular. Mozart's music does not have more power over us than other composers, his music has just been more studied.

Here are some of the physical benefits of music that closely relate to our study, as taken from *The Mozart Effect*.

Music slows down and equalizes brain waves[7].

Music can generate a sense of safety and well-being. The slower the brain waves, the more relaxed, contented and peaceful we feel.

Ordinary consciousness consists of *beta* waves which occur when we focus on daily activities, as well as when we experience strong negative emotions. Heightened awareness and calm are characterized by *alpha* waves. Listening to music with the beat of the music around 60-70 beats per minute can shift you from *beta* towards *alpha*, enhancing alertness, reducing stress and giving a sense of well-being.

Music affects respiration[8].

Breathing is rhythmic. As adults, we average eighteen breaths a minute. Deeper, slower breathing is better, contributing to calmness, control, and better metabolism. Listening to music around 60-70 beats per minute can alter one's breathing patterns and state of consciousness, harmonizing right and left sides of the brain. [9]

Music affects heartbeat, pulse rate and blood pressure[10].

The human heartbeat is particularly attuned to sound and music. Music is a natural pacemaker. Our heart responds to frequency, tempo and volume of the sounds that surround us. A slower heartbeat creates less physical tension and stress, calms the mind and *helps the body heal itself.*

On the other hand, excessive noise can change blood pressure by as much as 10%, may trigger the fight-or-flight mechanism, which causes adrenaline to be released, speeding up the heart and straining the blood vessels.[11]

Music reduces tension, improves body movement and coordination[12].

Dr. Thomas Verny notes that babies from week twenty-four gestation actually *keep rhythm* to the beat of music in utero.[13] We had known that babies move to rhythm *after birth*, but scientists have proven that *every baby has natural rhythm "built in" by God before they are born.* Muscle strength, flexibility and tone are influenced by sound and vibration.

Studies have shown that music increases strength, ability to pace movements, enhances mood and motivations while exercising.[15] Researchers show that music will reduce muscle tension and relax children with severe physical and mental disabilities.[16] In recovery wards and rehab clinics, music is used to restructure and "re-pattern" repetitive movements following accidents or illness.[17]

Music affects endorphin levels which boost the immune system[18].

Music can produce euphoria, a heightened sense of well-being. We also know it as the "runner's high."

Later in this manual, we will gave you criteria for baby-approved "preferred" music. There is a link between listening to/playing this "preferred music" and the secretions of endorphins which lessen pain and induce a "natural high." Researchers say that listening to "preferred music" for thirty minutes every day gives the same emotional lift as taking one sedative.[19]

Scientists found that "preferred music" may create a profound positive emotional experience that can lessen factors contributing to disease.

God created our body to work in harmony. When that is achieved, our body is successful in resisting disease. Endorphins, the healing chemicals created by the joy and emotional richness in music, enable the body to create its own anesthetic and enhances the immune function.[20] No one needs a boost in the immune system more than an expectant mom and a newborn baby. Current research in immunology suggest that insufficient oxygen in the blood may be a cause of immune deficiency and degenerative disease. Certain types of vocal music can actually oxygenate the cells. Here again we see the importance of singing!

Here are some related case studies:
- Vocal exercises increase the lymphatic circulation up to three times the normal rate.[21]
- Listening to music for only fifteen minutes could increase levels of interleukin-1 (IL-1) in the blood. (Interleukins are a family of proteins associated with blood and platelet production, lymphocyte stimulation and cellular protection against AIDS, cancer and other diseases. [22])
- Listening to "preferred music" drops levels of cortisol up to 25%. High levels of cortisol can lead to a decline in the immune response.[23]
- Natural endorphin highs may elevate the levels of T-cells, the lymphocytes that boost natural immunity to disease. T-cell decline is associated with AIDS/HIV infection, leukemia, herpes, mononucleosis, measles and other disorders.[24]
- Physiological measurements show that musical rhythms stimulate the release of endorphins and reduce blood levels of certain hormones (ACTH and prolatic) associated with stress.[25]

Music affects the need for medication and actually relieves pain[26].
- Because of the increased endorphin release, half of the expectant mothers who listen to music during childbirth do not require anesthesia. Music decreases the need for medication, provides a distraction from pain and relieves anxiety.[27]
- Surgery patients have significantly less pain after only two days using relaxation techniques and music. The music seems to interrupt the <u>transmission</u> of pain signals – reducing the actual amount of pain being felt, as well as creating calm. [28]

Music stimulates digestion[29].

Listening to music during and after you eat speaks peace to your digestive tract. A restaurant's choice of music will also influence how you eat, and how much you eat!
- Researchers found that rock music causes people to eat faster and to *eat more.*
- Classical music, especially slow string music, makes people eat more slowly, *consume less* <u>and</u> aids digestion.
- If you have a colicky baby, you need to play soothing, preferred music during and after his/her feedings as it may make a difference in their level of discomfort.

Just as music benefits the body ...

Music Benefits Our Souls

We could write volumes here, but we will show only the case studies that apply to our *Perfect Praise Baby* program.

Music helps establish emotional equilibrium[30].

Full term babies have more fully developed nervous systems and are more likely to exhibit an organized emotional state ... called emotional equilibrium.

♪ Nurses working with twenty newborns in a hospital nursery played classical music to full term babies, finding that they were far more likely to maintain their emotional equilibrium and maintain a state of relaxation, the exact opposite of the *stress response*. During control periods without the music, the babies were more likely to change back and forth between emotional states, often crying and being disoriented.

♪ Nurses at a NICU tried an experiment with preemies who were not exhibiting emotional equilibrium. They first spent ten minutes trying to calm the babies, then ten minutes using a taped recording of intrauterine (baby's prenatal environmental) sounds combined with a female voice singing, all while recording the babies heart rate, oxygen saturation and blood pressure. The babies experienced fewer episodes of oxygen deprivation and increased behavior equilibrium when the music played.[31]

Music strengthens memory and learning[32].

Studies show that your prenatal baby's brain is enhanced by an environment that includes baby-approved preferred styles of music. Here are the facts as we found them:
- Children exposed to "preferred" music in utero develop superior language skills, attention behaviors, could accurately imitate sounds made by adults, and have structured vocalizations earlier than the control group.[33]
- Sounds, rhythms and other forms of musical prenatal stimulation are not merely imprinted on baby's developing brain, but literally act to *shape* it.[34]
- The elements of music form the basis for the development of language such as pitch, phrasing, intonation, etc.[35]
- Prenatal exposure to Mozart improves temporal-spatial abilities *throughout his/her life.* [36]

These additional studies have to do with academic learning *after* birth.

- Playing light, easily-paced music helps us focus for longer periods of time, enhancing one's ability to memorize spelling, poetry and foreign words.[37]
- Early childhood musical experiences in the form of lullabies, musical mobiles and especially musical interactions where baby <u>is</u> <u>an</u> <u>active</u> <u>participant</u> aids in the development of the *neural networks* necessary for later processing.[38]
- College students who listen to Mozart score higher on IQ tests than control groups without such stimulation.[39]
- In a recent study, the top three nations in academic scores all have mandatory music requirements for their students. Hungary ranks top in academics. In Hungary, the first four hours of every day, children from K5 through 10th grade are required to study music. Then when they get to their academic studies, their brain has been formatted for orderly storage and retrieval of information, so they get good grades. Japan is number two and the Netherlands is number three in academic scores. In the Netherlands, music is a requirement for every student. They must pass a music proficiency exam prior to admittance to college.[40]
- Because of classical music's research regarding enhanced language, spatial and math skills, state-supported day care centers in Colorado, Georgia and Florida <u>require</u> that Mozart be played for their preschool children every day.[41]

Music enhances brain function.

With all that said, the most compelling proof yet to understand the mind of God regarding the intended and real impact of music is found in Psalm 49:1-4. *"Hear this all ye people; give ear all ye inhabitants of the world: Both low and high, rich and poor together. My mouth shall speak wisdom; and the meditation of my heart shall be of understanding. I will submit and consent to a parable or proverb; to the music of a lyre I will unfold my riddle (my problem).*

At first glance, this scripture seems heavy and elusive, so let's break it down.

This is for all people- *"all the inhabitants of the world."* This is for all classes of people- *"low and high"* (social), *"rich and poor"* (economic) ... together. Music will blend the classes. This is about *"wisdom."* This is about *"meditation."* Again, the words here are related to the musical art of musing. This is about *"understanding."* Meditation (musing) leads to understanding.

How do we arrive at wisdom, meditation, and understanding?

Verse four: with *"the lyre (or harp)"* that is by <u>participation</u> in music. The writer picks up a stringed instrument to play. He says, while I play my music, I will come to understand this parable; I will solve my problem.

"Parable" is a "byword, proverb, metaphor or simile." It comes from a root, which means *"to have or bear rule or dominion, reign, have power as a result of mental superiority."* In other words, a parable requires a sense of mental superiority to understand; the type of mental superiority that a ruler or governor, one with dominion, would possess.

So how do we figure out life's challenges? We play music.

Albert Einstein, Thomas Jefferson and Thomas Edison contributed their abilities to create and invent to music, as they wrote and invented things after extensive periods of practicing their instrument.[42]

Researchers concluded that music is the way out of poverty and being stuck in a "problem-riddled" lifestyle. This is also the answer to producing a society of entrepreneurs in a given region. The way to bring the whole world, rich and poor and high and low, together with the ability to understand, envision, produce and create … is through music.

Wow! That is *powerful*!

Let's move on.

Just as music benefits our body and our soul …

Music Benefits Our Spirit

You will not find <u>scientific</u> studies documenting that music affects our spirit … but we all know that it does. Music has power to bypass our physical body and soul and go straight to our heart.

How many times have you been "touched" by a song? It ministered to you, exactly what you needed, when you needed it. It's a touch that cannot be documented, but was there nonetheless.

Music's ability to stimulate our spirit is a major part of the power of music.

> The sounds with which you surround your child right now
> will make a difference in them for *eternity*.

An atheist was traveling in France with his wife.[43] He fell ill and was taken to a hospital, where he had what he described as an "out of body experience." Instead of going towards the light, as is often told, he was pulled towards a dark corridor by demons. They attacked him. Moments later, battered and beaten, torn and bleeding, he remembered words from his childhood … specifically, the song, "*Jesus loves me, this I know. For the Bible tells me so …* " (Traditional melody, public domain.)

He was so weak, all he could whisper was "*Jesus*." But each time he whispered that precious Name, the demons would jump back like His Name burnt their hands. Strength began to return to him as the demons fled. Angels brought him back to his room, where he called for a priest, who helped him accept Jesus as Savior. He totally recovered and now pastors a church in a North-Eastern state in the U.S.A.

This experience would have ended very differently if someone had not poured a simple children's song into him a long time ago. Many years later, hardened by the world and its pain, the lyrics came back to him. It made all the difference in his life for eternity, and now his life is contributing to that of countless others.

Through music's power,
you have the ability *right now* to pour into your child,
to strengthen his/her spirit life,
to create memories that will not fade;

memories that will be used by the Holy Spirit
when the time comes to draw your child to the Lord.

Right Brain, Left Brain or One Mind?

Albert Einstein's fifth grade teacher informed his parents that Albert was "stupid" and incapable of learning. His teacher recommended they remove him from school and place him in a workhouse. *And they did!* Yet Albert was later seen as the most brilliant man of the last century. What happened?

When asked to write the *Declaration of Independence* of the United States, Thomas Jefferson struggled to find the right words to express his heart. After many restless days and nights, *he gave up*. Yet we can hold in our hands an eloquently worded document penned by him. What happened?

In recent years, we have heard a lot about right brain and left brain. Doctors tell us that the right hemisphere is that which controls the emotional part of our thinking while the left hemisphere controls logic and reasoning.

The Bible doesn't mention right brain/left brain but says to have *"one mind."* (II Corinthians 13:11, James 1:8, 4:8)

Scientists have documented that music links the right/left hemispheres of the brain thereby creating *"one mind."* The trunk linking the hemispheres is thicker in musicians than in non-musicians. This thicker brain trunk represents higher learning circuitry.

Imagine your child's right brain/left brain as a connect-the-dots diagram. The dots represent neurons waiting to be connected by new pathways of information called neural bridges. Each time your child's mind is stimulated, either new neural bridges are formed or pre-existing ones are strengthened. The more bridges formed or strengthened, the more the intellect will be developed. The opposite is also true.

When a person from age six to eighty participates in piano activities, his/her *"one mind"* (left brain/right brain flowing together) lasts for four or five hours, formatting his/her brain for orderly storage/retrieval of information.

When a child under the age of five participates in bouncing, rhythmic and piano-based musical activities, his/her *"one mind"* lasts *for the rest of his/her life* because neural wiring is taking place linking the two hemispheres. This *"one mind"* gives the brain function enhancement that permits higher learning and reasoning skills; resulting in enhanced abilities in math, reading and science…the big subjects that academically contribute to successful lives.

Early Training

Our *Early Childhood Music*® (**ECM**) curriculum was first birthed due the music benefit research available in 1998. Now years later, our student graduates *provide* our music research. And it's incredible!

Perfect Praise, Inc. operates local *Early Childhood Music*® schools. We began tracking our **ECM**® graduates in 2004. We see several things in common in our students who use our Early Childhood Music® curriculum.

Our students have ability to sing and match pitch.
Very young children have natural window for ear training.

Babies who have received prenatal musical stimulation begin singing at an early age, almost as soon as they begin learning to speak.

The most current research we found showed that song babbling and spontaneous singing can be observed beginning around the age of six months.[44] The researchers also state that early singing is accurate in contour (patterns) but not pitch. Pitch accuracy usually begins to develop by age three ***years***, and children will not be able to sing the correct pitch for another few years.[45]

Totally blowing this research apart, our **ECM** students **do** match pitch at age three years and sometimes much earlier. Babies completing our **GTBS** prenatal program have been seen singing and matching pitch at age *three* and *four* ***months***.[46]

These incredible results have to do with their how their early training begins.

> When *musical concepts* are included in prenatal stimulation,
> accurate pitch and ear training may begin very early.

Here is another research project that agrees with our results.

Rosa Plaza,[47] a violinist, and her husband, a pianist, live in Valencia, Spain. During her pregnancy they were very musical, with Rosa practicing the violin four to five hours every day while Manuel played the piano. They attended concerts frequently.

After birth, their son began to sing musical scales at *six* months of age. He had amazing spatial reasoning sense, perfect pitch hearing, space-time relations skills and outstanding manual dexterity. He gave his first recital at age three for the National Radio of Spain. He began a series of performances which earned him the nickname of "the Mozart of Spain."

Our students read several grade levels above their peers.
Most of our graduates are seven to eight years old when they complete our **ECM** program. At that time, most of them read at 4th and 5th grade level, sometimes much higher.

Superior reading skills are seen by educators as one of the big three subjects that bring on enhanced academic scores. Reading skills expands their world and creates new horizons for learning in every area.

Our students are academically superior to their peers.
Since 2004, when we began tracking our graduate's academic excellence, all of our graduates receive straight A's in every academic subject if they started our program under the age of five.

All of the students who begin by age six get mostly straight A's, with an occasional B.

All of our students who began by age five (four years old or younger) get straight A's academically. Their favorite subjects are Math, Science and Reading, the big three that contribute to successful lives.

A picture hangs in the lobby of one of our schools, which depicts a grand piano surrounded by doctors, businessmen, ballerinas, baseball players, etc. The caption reads, *"Success in music, success in life ... it's no coincidence."* (Yamaha)

That caption says it all.

The characteristics that we want in our children's life are enhanced by music lessons, specifically piano-based lessons. But even beyond that, when your child plays the piano and sings, the right hemisphere and left hemisphere of his/her brain flows together, creating harmony, releasing and creating an atmosphere for creativity and learning.

And the foundation for that starts now. Pediatric neurobiologist Dr. Harry Chugani of Wayne State University says, "Early experiences are so powerful they can completely change the way a person turns out." He based this comment on scientific research and first-hand musical experiences with his child.[48]

Music lessons have been shown in one scientific research study after another to give the highest brain function enhancement when centered on the piano with singing.

We have been blessed to be able to demonstrate that when children ages three and four are provided the right elements in a piano training class and an early start in music exposure, they are able to learn to read and play piano by note, with singing, transpose and compose. And the younger they start, the better!

Our students are amazing musicians.

Even with all the years that we have taught piano, we are totally amazed at the abilities of our **ECM** students. By using the open windows of natural rhythm and ear training, *solfege* singing and partner-based classes, we witness amazing performing skills at the piano.

When they graduate our program they are able to play the piano in five different keys (three major and two minor), transpose and compose their own songs. They are able to play the keyboard by grand staff or lead sheets. They have a musical foundation that enables them to go into any instrument of choice at a very young age.

Our students are leaders in every area.

Once we first began tracking our graduates we discovered that they are leaders in every area of their life. Our graduating classes are filled with captains of their swim teams, baseball pitchers, swim team captains, state composition winners, six year old soloist at the local Opera, captain of the cheerleading squad, lead dancer in the local ballet, and on it goes. We have had seven-year olds play the piano for their Mother's wedding, grandparent's funeral, participate in nursing homes, lead worship for their local churches and perform on stage at their schools.

We could continue to list the attributes of these children but you get the point.

Due to the performance opportunities and the musicianship built into these children from a very young age, most are confident, poised, creative thinkers and natural leaders.

Our students face challenges with gusto.

We recently had the opportunity to work with several of our **ECM** graduates in private piano lessons.

These six to eight-year old graduates have another common denominator. This benefit has to do with how they approach a challenging piece of music.

A student raised in traditional piano lessons is usually overwhelmed by a challenging new piece of music. When given a new book, most shy away from the first songs and are petrified by the last ones.

Not these graduates! They jump in and eagerly seek the most difficult piece in the book. It's almost like the more challenge, the more the excitement and determination in their approach! And they succeed!

We believe that these children will grow up approaching life the same way, with a sense of eagerness and determination, not overwhelmed by life's obstacles … yet succeeding in every area. We believe that it's their early involvement with music that makes the difference.

In the Old Testament the word "musician" is used only in the headings of many of the Psalms. It comes from the Hebrew word "naw-tsakh." It means, "to glitter" and is used of *"one who is chief, who excels, one who is permanent."* What amazing adjectives to describe a musician.

It could be argued that these attributes refer directly to the fact that the word "naw-tsakh" is the English word "chief musician," with the emphasis on *chief. We believe, however, that the underlying thought here in the mind of God is that those appointed to the position of chief musician in David's tabernacle and referred to in Psalms were so appointed because they were musicians first.* They excelled and so were elevated to places of authority. They displayed leadership, were recognized and were appointed to lead. They showed the discipline to be permanent and, because it was felt they would complete an assigned task, they were given chief positions.

It is our contention that music, especially when explored in a child's early formative years, will impart a discipline and an order into his/her character that will be *permanent*. He/she will have the order and discipline needed to complete projects, be fulfilled and responsible.

> Music is like a circle of LOVE!
> God gives music to us to enhance us spirit, soul and body.
> We give it back to Him in worship and praise.
> <u>He</u> is glorified; <u>we</u> are enhanced, and <u>He likes it!</u>

Let's Recap...

1. Music allows our body to heal itself.
2. Music makes brain waves calm.
3. Music boosts the immune system.
4. Music lowers blood pressure.
5. Music lowers respiration.
6. Music stimulates digestion.
7. Music reduces stress and stress hormones.
8. Music enhances brain development.
9. Music improves coordination.
10. Music reduces muscle tension.
11. Music causes release of endorphins elevating mood.
12. Music relieves pain and the need for medication.
13. Music aids in achievement of emotion equilibrium.
14. Music generates a sense of safety and well-being.
15. Music strengthens learning and memory.
16. Music helps us focus, enhancing learning and ability to memorize.
17. Music creates neural networks necessary for processing science, math and engineering skills.
18. Music gives the desire to live to preemie babies.
19. Music gives ability to find solutions to life's difficulties.
20. Music permits us to worship our God.
21. Music unites across economic and social barriers.
22. Music expands us academically.
23. Music helps us reach our full potential.
24. Music creates leaders.
25. Music changes how we approach life's challenges.
26. Music causes one to be permanent.
27. Music does so much more!

Spiritually Impart
To Your
Perfect Praise Baby

Perfect Praise, Inc. believes that God has given parents the amazing opportunity to spiritually impart to your offspring. If you don't do it, who will? Parenthood is an amazing journey that began when your child was conceived.

Psychologists tell us the preschool years are the formative years… specifically to age five. God created the process called parenthood as an opportunity for imparting to the next generation.

It's fun to watch a toddler as they copy everything that their parent does. You are modeling for your child, whether you are aware of it or not. Choose to be all that you can be.

Here's why:
1. It is our belief that just as God, the Creator, speaks and all things are impacted, He has given you the precious ability to take part in His creative purpose in your baby. When you speak in agreement with Him your baby's destiny, contained in the Father's heart, is imparted into your baby. When you declare the Word of God over your baby, your baby is impacted for God and His purposes.
2. It is God's intent that by pronouncing God's Word over your baby, habits will develop in you as parents that will become set as daily routines of devotional habits of teaching your child God's Word. (Psalm 78:4-6; Deuteronomy 6:4-7). This is part of what God means when He says in Proverbs 22:6 "…train up a child in the way it should go, and when he is hold he will not depart from it."
3. When you speak, you produce sound waves and those waves penetrate everything they touch. As you speak the Word of God over your baby and into his/her genes those words *will* leave their mark. They will produce God's desired result in your baby. God's Word "…will not return unto Him void…" but *will* accomplish the thing He sent it out to do (Isaiah 55:11).
4. When you declare the Word of God, as in the form of a prayer, you are prophetically speaking into your baby's life. You are prophesying the already spoken Word of God. You are lining up in agreement, as parent of your child, with God and what He has decreed, and *it will come to pass* in your baby's life.

The Word of God, His seed, in your baby's heart and mind will not be stolen because your baby is being covered by the Creator. We believe this has to do with what we call the "age of accountability," or the age at which a child is "ready" to trust Jesus as Savior.

A child's brain is not completely formed until around age five or six. (God has created everyone as individual, so it varies slightly.) The younger you begin impartation, the better for your child.

"...Train up your child in the way it should go, when old he/she will not depart from it" (Proverbs 22:6). Proverbs 18:21 says that "...death and life are in the power of the tongue." **You,** Mom and Dad, have the power to impart by speaking life into your baby. Speak the things of God, the things of the Word of God and the things of faith into your baby on a daily basis.

You are setting the preferences for life for your baby. Protect their environment. Set an example by your behavior, words and attitudes.

Give your baby a hunger and thirst for God and His righteousness, for His Word, a hunger that will *never* be stolen by the enemy, because it was engrained in their genetic makeup. You are instilling it in them in from their very first days!

What an opportunity!

Sing To Your *Perfect Praise Baby*

Have you ever wondered why a woman's voice is pitched higher than a man's? Research shows that not only do prenatal babies *prefer* higher pitched sounds but they *need* higher decibels for their development.[49]

> What an awesome Creator!
> He created moms to have *high-pitched voices*
> and babies to *need* those higher decibels for proper development.

This is true prenatally and it is true after your baby is born. Your baby is emotionally aware and requires stimulation and love. *Singing to your baby is how you best convey your love and God's love.*

a.) Singing to your baby enhances *bonding*. Bonding with your baby started at conception. *Your voice is one of the most intimate and pleasurable events experienced by your baby both before and after birth.* Songs that communicate love and acceptance are the most reassuring to your baby.

b.) Singing to your baby enhances *communication*. Your baby is emotionally and intellectually connected to you. Singing enhances that communication.

c.) Your voice creates *memories*. Songs passed down from generation to generation soothe an irritable baby, especially if the songs have been sung to baby in utero. Sing those songs while you rock your baby. The familiar songs convey a sense of emotional comfort, bringing back pleasant memories of life experienced in the womb.

- The songs and music that are heard frequently before birth will be recognized after birth, especially when you *sing* them.
- Traditional lullabies, as well as *newly composed songs* by Mom and Dad, are personal musical expressions of love from parents to their baby. So, write your own lullaby.
- Nursery songs are remembered for a lifetime and form a soothing bond that comfort and reassure your baby.

Now more than ever, you need to be obedient to sing to the Lord. Worship Him with your voice, with thanksgiving, with the harp or lyre. (Psalm 147:7) Your baby will be the benefactor: spirit, soul and body.

Note: It's important not to let inhibitions regarding your inability to sing keep you from providing this for your baby. Focus on the Lord with your singing … not your ability *or* lack of it. Your baby doesn't judge you. *Your baby needs this stimulation.*

What To Sing

1. Scriptures: We encourage you to put your favorite scripture passages to music. "Sing it and you'll never forget it." It is a well known fact that if you want to memorize something … put it to music and *sing it*!

When you sing scriptures, your voice will ingrain these passages into your baby and they will "come back to them" when needed in their life.

2. *Solfege*: *Solfege* is an international musical singing language. You may be familiar with the song, "Doe a deer, a female deer …" Dating back to 950 A.D., *solfege* has been linked as an absolute means to develop the singing ear, to enhance pitch training and permits students to excel in musicianship.

3. With a Xylophone: In a related study, scientists placed a cancer cell under a microscope and played Ionian scales on a variety of instruments. When they played the xylophone, *the cancer cell totally annihilated itself in* **<u>fourteen</u>** *minutes!*

Experimenting with another uterine cancer cell, they played scales on a xylophone while a *woman's voice* sang *solfege. The cancer cell totally annihilated itself in* **<u>nine</u>** *minutes.* The researching doctor, Dr. Maman Fabien said, "The human voice carries something in its vibration that makes it more powerful than any musical instrument." [50]

In our *Perfect Praise Baby* classes, we introduce *solfege* as the forerunner to playing the piano. Babies in our **ECM** program match pitch as young as three and four <u>months</u> old after completing the prenatal **GTBS** program.

Based on this and other research, as well as the abilities personally witnessed in our very young *ECM* students, we include *solfege* singing in our *Perfect Praise Baby* program. <u>You</u> may begin today to enhance <u>your</u> child's ear-training with the xylophone and *solfege* singing at home. (You may order your xylophone today through *Perfect Praise Inc.*)

Create Soothing Surrounding Sounds
For Your
Perfect Praise Baby

Music researchers in the early 2000's reported that a prenatal baby is influenced by what mom listens to. That research was a foundation-stone for our *Give Them the Best Start (***GTBS***)* prenatal program.

Music research had already shown the benefit of listening to classical music. *Perfect Praise, Inc.* merged those two powerful research findings for our prenatal program and for *Perfect Praise Baby* program.

> Your baby, prenatal or already born,
> is greatly influenced by preferred
> classical styles of music.

Let's examine what, when, why and how.

What is classical music?

Classical music is music composed between 1600 A.D. and the late 1800's. It contains high voicing, patterns and order. Classical music was not called <u>classical</u> when it was written. Just as an old car past a certain age is known as a classic, this grouping of music has endured the test of time and is known as *classical*.

Classical music was composed by many people for many reasons, although much of it was written for church use. Classical music, at the time of its writing, was not popular because these new styles broke all the very rigid rules of music for that day. Based on what the researchers state regarding the benefits from this form of music, we believe that God anointed it to enhance our lives.

Listening to classical music has great benefits for people of any ages. However, music researchers note that <u>not</u> all forms of classical music enrich and benefit.

Baby– Approved (Preferred) Classical Styles

A parent enrolling her two-year old into one of our schools recently told that her child had just made a comment regarding a CD playing in the car.[51]

She said, "Mommy, that was my favorite song when I was in your tummy!" This remark came out of the blue as they had never discussed music in this way.

The child's Mom went on to share that she was forced to drive four hours weekly to an OB-GYN specialist during her last trimester. This child had received *inadvertent* prenatal music. The CD the child referenced was her Mom's favorite during those prenatal days. Her daughter remembered it two and a half years later, and even remembered her prenatal preferences for <u>one</u> song on the CD! *Amazing*!

Not only is *that* amazing, but this little girl is a remarkable child. After only two lessons in her toddler class, we promoted her into the 3-4 year old class because of her enhanced vocal and developmental skills. (She sang words to new songs, on pitch, her second lesson! That is *not* normal toddler ability!) Last month she performed her first recital. She played a piano solo, while singing the words … and she is still several months away from her *third* birthday! *That's amazing!*

This story is a dramatic demonstration that a child can remember his/her prenatal environment years later and has *preferences*. Your baby in utero is an emotionally aware, spiritually aware, physical person with all of his/her senses actively functioning by the sixth month; so even your newborn has an *opinion*.

Researchers has viewed ultrasounds while different styles of music are being played. They have documented that babies (prenatal and newborn) have an opinion regarding what they hear.

Researchers saw that babies seem to enjoy classical music from the Baroque period. The Baroque period is the period of time starting around 1600 A.D., ending in the mid 1700's. During the Baroque period, composers designed pieces that were especially decorative with lots of order and high voicing.

The most famous Baroque composers include Mozart, Beethoven, Bach and Handel. Even among these composers, you will find that babies seem to *prefer* the slower movements of their compositions. And researchers found that when baby is exposed to these slower styles the benefits *increase*.

This music has <u>more</u> power and is preferred by babies more than other styles. We find it amazing that the babies prefer the music that has the most benefit for them.

So what is it about this style of classical music that stimulates every cell and fiber of our being? Have you noticed the word that has already appeared several times in this section?

Order. Musical order. God's musical order.

God created *order* in our universe and His musical order holds our universe together. Music's patterns stimulate *and* calm our bodies, our souls and our spirits. Musical order touches us in ways nothing else can. God created it that way.

Researchers state that baby-approved preferred music should fit the following criteria:
1. **Repeated Patterns and Order:** The melody must have many repeated patterns and much order as our bodies respond to that order.[52]
2. **High Voicing:** Strings (piano and violin) are especially enjoyed. High-pitched sounds are preferred by very young babies and researchers say they seem to stimulate developing brain function the best.[53]
3. **Tempo:** The tempo (speed) of the song should be around 60-70 beats per minute. A person's heart rate adapts itself to the tempo of the music that they listen to. Generally the second movement of a classical piece is calmer and slower. This movement is preferred.
4. **Enjoyable**: Other than these three criteria, the music that you play for your baby should be enjoyable.

Preferred Music, When and Where

You should plan to <u>include</u> this style of music on a daily basis. That's not as difficult as it sounds. Here are some ideas:
- ♪ Put the CD player in your nursery and click it on when you got in to pick your baby up the first thing in the morning.
- ♪ Have it nearby when you are bathing your baby or changing his/her diaper.
- ♪ Put the CD in the car and play it when your baby gets tired or fussy.
- ♪ Play it in the evening as part of your 'wind-down' activities for the evening.
- ♪ Play it during nap time.

Researchers state that you should not play music to your child 24/7. We agree.

Here is a case study from our archives:

A band teacher worked with us a few years ago.[54] He and his wife were aware of the power of the prenatal environment. When they knew they were pregnant, they set a guard around their baby's prenatal sanctuary. Mom did not listen to anything but Christian and/or classical music. She did not listen to the radio and did not watch TV. After his birth, they played the *Baby Mozart CD* 24/7 in their son's environment for his first *four years*.

Why four years? Because one night the power went off and the music stopped. Mom noticed that her son's behavior was calmer the next day. She experimented and found it to be true that her son was calmer during the day following no music. So she put a stop to the night recordings and just continued during the daytime.

We met this family when this little boy was five years old. His development is truly remarkable. He later skipped kindergarten and first grade and was placed directly into 2nd grade as a five year old. They have since had his IQ tested and he is a genius.

There are styles of music that will overly stimulate. We believe that if you select the styles of music that we have set the criteria for, you will not overly stimulate your baby.

While researchers tell us that babies respond best to high pitched sounds and calm, orderly music, they react adversely to loud/heavy music. Music has great power ... for the good and for the bad. Be selective and choosey. You can change your entire household's atmosphere by changing what is coming out of the CD player.

Perfect Praise, Inc. has compiled a short list of approved classical pieces. This is only a sampling of what is available. However, once you hear these selections, you will have a better idea of how to select titles from your own CD collections.

Note: All of these titles came from a collection called **Classical Relaxation Recordings.**[55] Contact *Perfect Praise, Inc.* for more information regarding acquiring this wonderful CD collection.

- Beethoven: Minuet
- Bizet: Carmen Suite #1
- Chopin: Piano Concerto No. 2 (Larghetto)
- Haydn: Serenade, Op. 3 No. 5
- Rheinberger: Evening Song
- Mendelssohn: Notturno

- Mozart: Flute Quarter in G Major
- Mozart: Symphony No. 35 "Haffner"
- Mozart: Symphony No. 36 "Linz"
- Mozart: Eine kleine Nachtmusik Romance
- Mozart: Sinfonia Concertante in E Flat Major (Andante)
- Schubert: Piano Sonata in B flat Major (Andante)
- Tchaikowsky: Swan Lake

Remember: To adequately stimulate your developing baby, *it is important to listen to baby-approved preferred classical music **every** day.*

Here is another first-hand testimony from one of our families.[56] This man was born in the 1960's before scientists were even aware of the benefit of listening to classical music. His mom, by accident or by plan, surrounded him with classical music before *and* after birth.

Now in his early 40's, this gentleman's IQ is in the 160's. He has created and patented several inventions for NASA. He currently owns his own aerospace company and two other companies. He is a very gifted musician, writes his own music, playing every instrument that he picks up.

Since this family is aware of the benefit of listening to classical music, they made sure that *their* baby had prenatal music. During their pregnancy, Dad was writing and creating an instrumental CD. His wife joined him in the music room most evenings since this project consumed much of their spare time. Their prenatal baby heard the same songs over and over.

After birth, the new CDS power over their newborn quickly became apparent. Just the first two or three notes of the first song would quickly gain his total attention and calm him.

This little boy began speaking at eight months and had a vocabulary of 250+ words by eighteen months. At age two years, he understands shapes such as octagon, parallelogram, hexagon, parabola, and trapezoid.

Praise and Worship Music

In addition to classical music, you should surround your baby with soothing instrumental praise and worship music.

Praise and worship has a calming effect over your baby, because, again, your baby feels what you feel. Baby picks up the stress release that worship gives *you* and God is glorified in the process.

1. **Instrumental Praise CDS:** We encourage you to worship everyday with instrumental CDS and with soft, soothing worship songs.
2. **Classical Styled Worship:** Visit your Christian bookstore and look for praise and worship songs performed in a classical style. Then enjoy the slower selections.
3. **Relaxation CDS** with environmental sounds should also be enjoyed and will calm everyone.

Perfect Praise's Classical Praise CD

Perfect Praise Baby gives you a head start in choosing baby-approved preferred classically styled praise selections. Songs recorded on our *Classical Praise CD* were chosen for their calming nature and order.

Classical Praise CD is available through *Perfect Praise Inc.*

Bounce
Your
Perfect Praise Baby

Bouncing your baby probably dates back to the Adam and Eve because moms know instinctively to sing, rock and bounce their babies. Recent scientific music research shows us the benefits of this stimulation.

Ms. Laurel Trainor, a psychologist in Canada, observed parents bouncing their babies and led a research study to investigate the benefits of this movement. Her study involved sixteen seven-month old babies. She had them listen to rhythm patterns made by a snare drum and sticks. Half of the moms bounced their babies on counts one and three of a march pattern, and the other half bounced on the first count of a waltz pattern. She played the patterns again, this time without bouncing, and measured the amount of time they paid attention to the stereo speakers.[57]

The babies showed that they preferred the pattern that their mother bounced them to… ignoring the other pattern. Follow-up tests with blindfolded babies gave the same result, showing that vision was not important to this sensory development.

This study and many like it, indicates that <u>active</u> involvement with music wires the sensory system. The type of development enhanced relates to language, communication and perceptual skills. Passive listening to music, while calming and enjoyable for your baby, doesn't bring about the sensory stimulation that <u>active</u> involvement achieves. So music researchers are trumpeting the need for active exposure to all styles of music.

Blanket baby:
- *If your baby is fussy, sing the songs that you sang while your baby was in-utero. Rock and cuddle your baby. Listening to prenatal music now will remind your baby of safe times and will bring comfort.*
- *Dance around the room holding your baby in the cradle or burp position. Bounce slightly up and down. Sing songs with different rhythms and styles.*

Lap baby:
- *Continue singing to your baby as before.*
- *When baby is old enough to hold up his/her head, turn them to face forward and continue to bounce to your favorite tunes. Add a rattle or maraca. Do*

these activities in front of a mirror.
- *Put your baby in a jumper or walker. Surround them with music. They will bounce themselves… to the beat.*

Walking baby:
At this age, babies become very independent and may not enjoy lap bounces as much as before. That's okay, sneak one in every chance you get. When your child becomes a toddler, he/she will once again enjoy lap bounces.

Read
To Your
Perfect Praise Baby

Your baby has its first language lesson from Mom prenatally, picking up the cadence of her language.

Mom has a wonderful prenatal opportunity to impart truth, Godly wisdom and life to her unborn baby.

Both parents have that opportunity after birth.

Parents, you have an awesome opportunity to affect your child's preferences and Godly beliefs. Whatever you pour into them right now stays with them for life!

We encourage you to read to your baby, especially your favorite scriptures and children's books with moral codes. You are imparting life to them; be choosey!

Creating Musical Experiences For Your
Perfect Praise Baby

Lullabies
♪ Sing lullabies to your baby while holding and rocking them. Sing songs that you sang during the prenatal days. As your baby grows independent, give him/her a stuffed toy to rock while you rock them.

Suggested selections from this book: *Snuggle Up with Me, Hush Little Baby, God is So Good.*

Sing While Feeding Your Baby
♪ Sing to your baby while you feed him/her. Sing songs praising God. Build a foundation for the future spiritual growth of your child.
♪ Singing bonds baby to parent. Rock your baby as you sing as this will make this time more precious.

Suggested selections from this book: *Snuggle Up With Me, God is So Good, Kum Ba Ya.*

Music Chants While Changing The Diaper
♪ Some babies voice their frustration when having their diaper changed. Music chants and taps can make this time special.
♪ Use rhythmic massage rhythms when applying lotion or creams to your baby.

Suggested selections from this book: *One Leg Two Leg, Wash the Dishes, Round and Round the Garden.*

Sing and Cuddle Your Baby
♪ One of the basic needs of every baby is to be held and cuddled. Music can enhance cuddling for all involved.
♪ Your baby prefers the voice of the parent's to all other voices. If your baby is restless or fussy, your voice has the ability to calm your child.

Suggested selections from this book: *Hush Little Baby* and *Snuggle Up With Me.*

Family Members and Babysitters Sing to the Baby
♫ Your baby recognizes the voices of family members. Parents, babysitters, grandparents and older siblings should sing at every opportunity. Babies prefer female and unchanged male voices to changed male voices. However, everybody can and needs to sing to the baby.

Massage Your Baby
♫ If a baby has all his physical needs provided, but is not held or cuddled, *he will die* as touch is vital for your baby's emotional and physical growth. We have included massage rhymes for you use to love on your baby. Your baby will respond to your love.

Suggested selections from this book: *Two Little Eyes, A Little Flea Went Walking.*

Sing While Bathing Your Infant
♫ Make bath time a pleasant experience by singing to your baby.

Suggested selections from this book: *Rub-A Dub-Dub* and *Wash the Dishes (substitute the word "baby" for "dishes").*

Massage Rhymes at Bath Time
♫ Massage rhymes soothe and relax your baby at bath time.
♫ These may also be used as you apply lotions or powders.
♫ Be sure to keep your chants rhythmical.

Suggested selections from this book: *Round and Round the Garden, Little Fire Fighters.*

Sing While Dressing Your Baby
♫ Babies often cry when parents dress them because they are either uncomfortable or sleepy.
♫ Singing to your baby while dressing him/her will make the experience pleasant for both of you.

Suggested selections from this book: *Jack & Jill, Two Little Apples, God is So Good.*

Musical Crib Toys
♪ Thankfully, baby toy manufacturers are getting on board with the music benefits research. **PPI** encourages you to have a musical toy in your baby's crib to promote growth and development. It also soothes them to sleep. When traveling take your musical crib toy as it will bring familiarity to them in strange surroundings.

♪ You must also play your *Perfect Praise Baby* CD and *Classical Praise CD* in their nursery.

Playing Musical Instruments for Your Baby
♪ If you play a musical instrument such as a flute, clarinet, piano, violin, or cello, bring your baby into the room while practicing.

♪ Your baby will particularly enjoy the high-pitched instruments.

Environmental Sounds.
♪ Baby moves in rhythm to the sounds around them and need the opportunity to hear. Take your baby with you as you move from room to room talking with family members and doing chores. Be aware of TV shows, music and other surrounding sounds.

♪ You have the power to bring comfort to your baby by being aware of what you are listening to.

Rhythmic Chanting
♪ Your baby needs to hear the sound of adult voices as often as possible to help lay the proper foundation for language development.

♪ Parents, nursery workers, babysitters, and day-care workers should chant Bible verses. This not only gives them opportunities to respond with movement to the sounds, but also helps lay the foundations for moral and spiritual development.

Reading To Your Baby
♪ Even though your baby has not developed communicative language skills, you should continue reading books as you did before your baby was born. Reading helps develop speech patterns.

♪ Read the Bible, poetry, children's books and stories that have a positive moral code.

Listen to Classical Music
♪ Play preferred classical music daily. Studies show that this type of rhythmical

patterns enhance brain function even while they sleep. We don't, however, recommend playing music all night as it may over-stimulate your baby.

Rock Your Child to Preferred Music
♪ Rock your baby while sitting in a rocking chair and listening to your favorite CD or worship music.
♪ Hum or sing the melody to comfort your baby.

Walking the Floor with a Colicky baby?
♪ If your baby has a tummy ache or colic, try a warm bath and soothing massage rubs on his tummy and back.
♪ Hold your baby in burp position and walk in rhythm to your favorite song, lullaby, or circle dance.
♪ Play preferred classical music in your baby's environment as it will soothe your baby. A musical swing helps greatly.

Suggested selections from this book: *Shoe a Little Horse, Hush Little Baby*

Listening to Familiar Music
♪ Whatever music you played in your prenatal months will be remembered by your baby even after birth.
♪ If you participated in the **GTBS** prenatal stimulation program, play your **GTBS Activity CD** even after birth. Your baby will remember and be calmed.

Name Recognition
♪ Very early, baby begins to recognize and respond to their name.
♪ Songs and chants in which their names can be inserted reinforce name recognition.

Suggested selections from this book: *Whoops Johnny, Pat-a-Cake.*

Travel Time
♪ Being strapped into a car seat can make a baby very unhappy. Music helps soothe this frustration. It is a wonderful opportunity for parents to use their *Perfect Praise Baby* CD and their favorite songs to restore calmness. Your baby will let you know what they like… tune in!

Developmental Stages
Of Your
Perfect Praise Baby

Because of the vast changes that occur in a child from newborn to age eighteen months, our *Perfect Praise Baby* book's activities are shown with three baby development stages:

Blanket Baby: A *blanket baby* is a baby who is content to lie on a blanket. This would include a newborn until he/she begins to crawl.

Lap Baby: A *lap baby* is defined as one who is sitting up, holding his/her head up but not yet walking.

A walking baby who is content to be held is still considered a lap baby and may enjoy many chants and songs from this position.

Walking Baby: A *walking baby* is a child who is no longer content to be held in your lap.

A walking baby is toddling about and gaining independence.

Note: Even after your child has passed a stage, he/she might still enjoy certain activities from the prior stage.

Lullabies and Rocking Songs
For Your
Perfect Praise Baby

As every mother knows, a soothing lullaby can be just what the doctor ordered for a fussy or sleepy baby. Rocking your baby should be a part of the bedtime rituals in every home.

Usually if begun early enough, it will be enjoyed by your baby and looked forward to as a special time. Parents should sing when rocking your baby as your voice soothes and enhances your child.

Music will help make the transition from family time to bedtime smoother for your child. Include listening to a calm, soothing CD of '*Preferred Music*' as a part of your child's bedtime ritual.

Try these rocking positions with your baby.

Blanket Baby:
- ♪ *Cradle your baby in your arms and rock side to side while standing.*
- ♪ *Hold your baby in the burp position while you sway and sing.*

Lap Baby:
- ♪ *Rock your baby in a rocking chair.*

Walking Baby:
- ♪ *Place your baby on a hobbyhorse and rock gently to music.*
- ♪ *Give your baby a stuffed toy and let him rock the toy as you rock him/her.*

Hush Little Baby

Traditional Song #1

Hush little baby,
Don't say a word.
Papa's (or Mama's) going to buy you a mocking bird.
If that mocking bird don't sing,
Papa's going to buy you a diamond ring.
If that diamond ring turns brass,
Papa's going to buy you a looking glass.
If that looking glass gets broke,
Papa's going to buy you a Billie goat.
If that Billie goat runs away.
Papa's going to love you anyway.
Hush little baby,
Don't say a word.
Papa's (or Mama's) going to buy you a mocking bird.

God Is So Good

Song #2

God is so good.
God is so good.
God is so good.
He's so good to me.

He loves you so.
He loves you so.
He loves you so.
He's so good to you.

Snuggle Up With Me
Song by Denie Riggs
◎#3

Snuggle up with me
In the rocking chair.
Snuggle up with me,
Won't you please?
Snuggle up with me
In the rocking chair.
I love you.

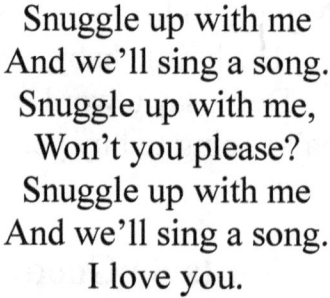

Snuggle up with me
And we'll sing a song.
Snuggle up with me,
Won't you please?
Snuggle up with me
And we'll sing a song.
I love you.

Snuggle up with me
And we'll go to sleep.
Snuggle up with me,
Won't you please?
Snuggle up with me
And we'll go to sleep
I love you. I love you.

Kum Ba Ya

Traditional Song #4

Kum ba ya, my Lord.
Kum ba ya.
Kum ba ya, my Lord.
Kum ba ya.
Kum ba ya, my Lord.
Kum ba ya.
Oh Lord, Kum ba ya.

Come by here, my Lord.
Come by here.
Come by here, my Lord.
Come by here.
Come by here, my Lord.
Come by here.
Oh, Lord, Come by here.

The Rocking Song

Traditional Song #5

Rocking, rocking, loo, loo, loo, loo, loo.
Rocking, rocking, loo, loo, loo, loo, loo.
Softly, softly sing with me.
Softly, softly sing with me.
Rocking, rocking, loo, loo, loo, loo, loo.

Lullaby Time
Traditional Song #6
Sleep baby sleep.
Sleep baby sleep.
Bye Lo, Bye Lo,
Sleep baby sleep.

Alleluia
Traditional Song #7
Alleluia, Alleluia, Alleluia, Alleluia, Alleluia
Alleluia, Alleluia, Alleluia, Alleluia, Alleluia

God is Love
Song by Denie Riggs #8
©2004
God is love. God is love.
God send Jesus for us now.
God is love, God is love
For this Gift we humbly bow.

God is love. God is love.
God send <u>baby</u> for us now.
God is love, God is love
For this gift we humbly bow.

From the Womb
Song by Denie Riggs ⊛ #9
©2004

From the womb I'll look for love
Searching for my God above.
Holy Father, may it be…
From the womb, I'll look to Thee.

From the womb, Thy will be done
Holy Father, Spirit, Son
Guide me, lead me in Thy way…
From the womb through every day.

Butterflies Flap Their Wings
Song by Denie Riggs ⊛ #10
©2004

Butterflies flap their wings
Little flowers lift their faces.
All of God's creatures down below
Are lifting up God's praises.

Little birds fly and sing,
Kangaroos run their races,
All of God's creatures down below
Are lifting up God's praises.

Jesus Loves Me
Traditional Song 🔘#11
©2004

Jesus loves me
This I know
For the Bible
Tells me so.
Little ones to Him belong
They are weak,
But He is strong.

Yes, Jesus loves me.
Yes, Jesus loves me.
Yes, Jesus loves me
The Bible tells me so.

Jesus Loves The Little Children
Traditional Song. Additional lyrics by Denie Riggs ❦ *#12*
©2004

Jesus loves the little children.
All the children of the world.
Red and yellow; black and white.
They are precious in His sight.
Jesus loves the little children of the world.

Jesus loves our little <u>baby</u>.
All the babies in the world.
Red or yellow; black or white.
All are precious in His sight.
Jesus loves the little <u>baby</u> in our world.
Jesus loves the little babies in the world.

(Substitute your baby's name for <u>baby</u>.)

Massage Rhymes
For Your
Perfect Praise Baby

Touch is the primary learning mode for your baby. Touching your baby helps develop sensory motor skills and is required for their proper development.

Massage rhymes are especially enjoyed at bedtime and bath time.

Try these massage techniques.

- ♪ *Gently move hands, paddle-wheel style, on baby's tummy.*

- ♪ *Use hand-over-hand motion gently on your baby's legs and arms.*

- ♪ *Move hands, paddle-wheel style in a circular motion on baby's tummy or back.*

- ♪ *Gently tap the beat of the chant while your fingers walk up your baby's arm or leg.*

Little Hot Dog
Traditional Chant
My father was a butcher
My mother cuts the meat.
And I'm a little hot dog
That runs around the street.

Blanket Baby:
♪ *Use the paddlewheel on the baby's tummy.*

Lap Baby:
♪ *Use the paddlewheel on the baby's tummy and goose on last line.*

Walking Baby:
♪ *Use as a floor game when you can catch them. Goose on last line.*

Fresh As the Dew
Massage Rhyme by Denie Riggs
©2004

Fresh as the dew
Our little love,
Heaven's treasure
Dropped from above.
Into our hearts
Forever to stay
We'll love and protect you
Every day.

Blanket Baby:
♪ *Use as a massage rhyme on your baby's back or tummy.*

Lap Baby:
♪ *Use as a lap bounce or while applying lotion to him/her.*

Walking Baby:
♪ *Hold your baby facing you. Bounce gently with the beat. Hug on last two lines.*

One Leg, Two Leg
Traditional Chant
One leg, two leg
Hot cross buns.
One leg, two leg
Isn't this fun?

Blanket Baby:
♪ *Rhythmically stroke baby's legs, (paddle wheel) hand-over-hand while applying lotion.*

Lap Baby:
♪ *This massage rhythm is great before bed or at bath time. While baby lies on a blanket in diaper only, pat a **steady** beat with simple movement.*

Walking Baby:
♪ *Same as for lap baby, and if your baby is alert and happy, you might want to tickle on 'isn't this fun?'*

Wash the Dishes
Traditional Chant
Wash the dishes, wash the dishes,
Ring the bell for tea,
Three good wishes, three good kisses,
I will give to thee.
One, two, three.

Blanket Baby:
♪ *Rhythmically stroke the tummy on first line...paddle wheel (hand-over-hand) while applying lotion.*

Lap Baby:
♪ *Rhythmically stroke the tummy on first line... paddle wheel (hand-over-hand.) Run finger down forehead and bounce off the nose on 'tea' and 'thee'. Kiss on each side of the cheek on 'one' and 'two' then kiss the tummy on 'three'.*

Walking Baby:
♪ *Hold your baby in your lap facing you. Taking the child's hands, roll arm over arm on 1st line. Clap on 2nd and 3rd line. Kiss on 'one,' 'two,' and goose the tummy on 'three.'*

Round and Round the Garden
Traditional Chant
Round and round the garden
Like a teddy bear.
One step, two step,
Tickle you under there.

Blanket Baby:
♪ *Lay your baby on a blanket and use the paddlewheel motions as you apply lotion after bath.*

Lap Baby:
♪ *Lay your baby on a blanket. Make a circle with paddlewheel motion on your baby's tummy or palm of his/her hand as you say the first line. Let your fingers walk up the tummy and tickle under the arm.*

Walking Baby:
♪ *Make a circle in the palm of your baby's hand. Walk up the arm on the 3rd line. Goose on last line.*

A Little Flea Went Walking
Traditional Chant
A little flea went walking
To see what he could see.
And all that he could see
Was <u>Baby's</u> little tummy.

♪ *Substitute your child's name for <u>baby.</u>*

Blanket Baby:
♪ *Use the paddlewheel on the baby's tummy or back. Gently stroke his/her cheek as your rock.*

Lap Baby:
♪ *Use the paddlewheel on the baby's tummy. Tickle towards the chin on the last line.*

Walking Baby:
♪ *Use as a lap bounce with your baby facing you. Goose on the last line.*

Two Little Eyes
Traditional Chant
Two little eyes to look around
Two little ears to hear each sound.
One little nose to smell what's sweet
And one little mouth that likes to eat!

Blanket Baby:
♪ *Lay your baby on a blanket. Stroke the baby's face as you name the body parts.*

Lap Baby:
♪ *Lay your baby on a blanket. Stroke the baby's face as you name the body parts:*

> *'Two little eyes to look around' …massage the forehead and around the eyes.*
> *'Two little ears to hear each sound'…around the ears and the chin.*
> *'One little nose to smell what's sweet'…come down the nose.*
> *'And one little mouth that likes to eat'…make a smiley face. First touch across the top lip then draw a big grin underneath.*

Walking Baby:
♪ *Use as a lap bounce with your child facing you.*

Criss-Cross Applesauce

Traditional Chant
Criss-cross applesauce.
Spider crawling up your back.
Cool breeze, tight squeeze.
And now you've got the shivers.

Blanket Baby:
♪ *Use the paddlewheel motion as you apply lotion following a bath or at bedtime.*

Lap Baby:
♪ *Massage rhyme: paddle wheel. Follow words. May also be used as lap bounce.*

Walking Baby:
♪ *Baby is sitting in diaper with the partner behind him.*
  Make an X across the back on the first line.
  Spider - fingers crawling up the back.
  Cool breeze - partner blows across baby's back.
  Give a hug on 'tight squeeze.'
  Tickle on 'the shivers.'

Round and Round the Haystack
Traditional Chant
Round and round the haystack.
Went the little mouse.
One step, two steps,
To his little house.

Blanket Baby:
♪ *Use the paddlewheel on your baby's tummy or gently stroke your baby's cheek as you rock and cuddle at bedtime.*

Lap Baby:
♪ *Use the paddlewheel on your baby's tummy. Tickle towards the chin on the last line.*

Walking Baby:
♪ *Use as a lap bounce with your child facing you. Goose on the last line.*

Little Angel Mine
Massage Rhyme by Denie Riggs
©2004

Little angel mine
I love you all the time…
I squeeze you, please you, tease you, seize you.
Little angel mine.

Little angel mine
I love you all the time…
I rub you, dub you, scrub you, hug you.
Little angel mine.

Blanket Baby:
♫ *Softly caress your baby's cheek as he/she is falling asleep.*

Lap Baby:
♫ *Use the paddlewheel on your baby's tummy.*
♫ *Use as a lap bounce with your child facing you or towards the group.*

Walking Baby:
♫ *Use as a lap bounce with your child facing you. Do appropriate movement as indicated by the words.*

Diaper Change Games
For Your
Perfect Praise Baby

Diaper change time is a special time that occurs for even the most active baby. No matter their development stage, or how much independence he/she has gained, they have to succumb for a fresh diaper.

This is your opportunity to have fun with diaper games. Diaper games will make this time enjoyable for all involved!

Blanket Baby:
- ♪ *Place your baby on a blanket and use the chant as a massage rhyme.*
- ♪ *Gently tap your baby's feet together to the rhythm of the chant.*

Lap Baby:
- ♪ *Use as lap bounce with your child facing you or towards the group.*
- ♪ *When changing the diaper, gently tap your baby's feet together to the rhythm of the chant.*

Walking Baby:
- ♪ *Use as floor games*

Going On A Bike Ride
Traditional Song #13
Going on a bike ride.
Going on a bike ride.
Going on a bike ride.
Who do you see?
<u>Baby's</u> on a bike ride.
Baby's on a bike ride.
Baby's on a bike ride.
Riding with me.

Substitute child's name or make up your own words.

Blanket Baby:
♪ *Lay baby on his/her back on a blanket. Gently take hold of your baby's ankles and make the motion of riding a bike. Stop at the end of each verse. This makes a great activity for diaper change time.*

Lap Baby:
♪ *Hold your child in your lap facing you. Use his/her arms for movement.*
♪ *During a diaper change, tap the bottom of feet together to the rhythm of the chant.*

Walking Baby:
♪ *Hold your child in your lap facing you or towards the group. Use as a lap bounce.*

Shoe A Little Horse
Traditional Chant
Shoe a little horse
Shoe a little mare
With a tap, tap here
And a tap, tap there.
Shoe a little horse
Shoe a little mare
But let the little colt go
Bare, bare, bare.

Blanket Baby:
♪ *Lay your baby on his/her back on a blanket. Tap the soles of their feet together with the beat of the chant. On the last line, tickle their tummy in rhythm on 'bare.'*

Lap Baby:
♪ *Lay your baby on his/her back on a blanket. Tap the soles of their feet together with the beat of the chant. On the last line, tickle their tummy in rhythm on 'bare.'*

Walking Baby:
♪ *Position your child in your lap facing you. Use this chant as a lap bounce with a goose on the last line.*

Roly-Poly, Roly-Poly
Traditional Chant
Roly-poly, Roly-poly up, up, up.
Roly-poly, Roly-poly down, down, down.
Roly-poly, Roly-poly, out, out, out.
Roly-poly, Roly-poly, in, in, in.

Blanket Baby:
♫ When changing your baby's diaper, use as a massage rhyme.

Lap Baby:
♫ Place your baby on a blanket, or when changing your baby's diaper, gently hold your baby's hands and do the appropriate movement.

Walking Baby:
♫ Hold your baby facing you. Hold his/her hands and do the appropriate movement. Tickle on the last "in."

Peek-A-Boo!
Traditional Song ☉#14
Peek-a-boo, Peek-a-boo.
I see you, I see you.
Peek-a-boo, Peek-a-boo.
Can you see me too?

Blanket Baby:
♪ *Very young babies do not like things over their face. Do this as a massage rhyme when changing the diaper.*
♪ Gently tap the bottom of your baby's feet together to the rhythm of the chant.

Lap Baby:
♪ Lightly place a scarf over your baby's head. Bounce it off on the last 'Peek-a-boo!'

Walking Baby:
♪ Place a scarf over <u>your</u> face. Let your baby pull it off... when you say, Peek-a-boo!

Peek-A-Boo! I See You!
Traditional Song ☻#15
Peek-a-boo
I see you,
Hiding in your place.
Peek-a-boo
I see you,
With your smiling face.
(Spoken) Peek-a-boo! I see you!

Blanket Baby:
♪ *Very young babies do not like things over their face. Do this as a massage rhyme when changing the diaper.*

Lap Baby:
♪ *Put the scarf lightly over your baby's face. Gently lift it off on the last 'Peek-a-boo!'*

Walking Baby:
♪ *Place scarf over your face. Let the baby pull it off... say, 'Peek-a-boo!'*

Gray Squirrel

Traditional Song #16
Gray Squirrel, Gray Squirrel
Swish your bushy tail.
Gray Squirrel, Gray Squirrel
Swish your bushy tail.
Wrinkle up your little nose.
Hold a nut between your toes.
Gray Squirrel, Gray Squirrel
Swish your bushy tail.

Blanket Baby:
♪ *Very young babies do not like things over their face. Do this as a massage rhyme when changing the diaper.*
♪ *Gently tap the bottom of your baby's feet together to the rhythm of the chant.*

Lap Baby:
♪ *Use as a massage rhyme or a lap bounce. Touch your baby's nose and toes at the appropriate time.*

Walking Baby:
♪ *Hold your child facing you. Move to the beat with the chant as a lap bounce. Touch their nose and toes at the appropriate time.*

Our Prayers Touched Heaven
Rhyme by Denie Riggs
©2004

Our prayers touched heaven
On the day you were conceived.
Our prayers will touch heaven
On the day that you'll believe
Jesus Christ was sent to die…
Through His blood you're glorified.
For His purpose you're alive …
Our prayers touched heaven!

Blanket Baby:
- ♪ *Place your baby on a blanket. Tap the bottom of your child's feet together rhythmically.*
- ♪ *Use as a massage rhyme.*

Lap Baby:
- ♪ *Using this chant as a lap bounce with your child facing you or towards the group.*

Walking Baby:
- ♪ *Use as a floor game.*

There's A Cobbler
Traditional Chant

There's a cobbler down the street
Mending shoes for little feet.
With a bang and a bang, and a bang, bang, bang.
Mending shoes the whole day long
Mending shoes to make them strong.
With a bang and a bang, and a bang, bang, bang.

Blanket Baby:
- ♪ *Lay your baby on a blanket. Tap the bottom of your child's feet together rhythmically.*
- ♪ *Use as a massage rhyme.*

Lap Baby:
- ♪ *Using this chant as a lap bounce, bounce your baby to the beat and clap your child's hands together on 'bang.'*

Walking Baby:
- ♪ *Use as a floor game.*

Kick Your Little Foot
Traditional Song, Lyrics by Denie Riggs 🎵 *#17*
©2004

<u>Kick your little foot</u>,
Kick your little foot
Kick your little foot with me.
Kick your little foot,
Kick your little foot
Kick your little foot with me.

And around we will go…
Not too fast, nor too slow.
And around we will go.
Not too fast, nor too slow.

Substitute: <u>Clap your little hands</u>… make up your own words.

Blanket Baby:
- ♪ *Lay your baby on a blanket. Tap the bottom of your child's feet together rhythmically.*
- ♪ *Use as a massage rhyme.*

Lap Baby:
- ♪ *Using this chant as a lap bounce, bounce your baby to the beat. On chorus, make circle on your baby's tummy.*

Walking Baby:
- ♪ *Use as a floor game.*

Wiggles
For Your
Perfect Praise Baby

Babies toes and fingers are so sweet. They are also great opportunities for developing rhythms and memories.

Baby's Finger Play
Chant by Denie Riggs, Copyright 2004
Here is your thumb, number one.
And pointer's number two.
I'll love on tall man, ring man, pinky …
'Cause they belong to *you!*

Toe Play Chant
Chant by Denie Riggs 2004
This little toe is big,
And this little toe is small
Three little toes in the middle…
And <u>Jesus</u> loves them all!

(Substitute <u>Mama</u> or <u>Daddy</u> etc.)

Blanket Baby:
- ♪ Place your baby on a blanket. Chant rhyme as you massage each toe or finger.

Lap Baby:
- ♪ Place your baby on a blanket, or when changing the diaper, kiss each little toe and finger.
- ♪ Hold your baby facing you and gently twist each toe or finger as you chant. "Goose" on the last line.

Walking Baby:
- ♪ Hold your baby facing you. Gently twist each toe or finger and do appropriate movement with the words. "Goose" on the last line.

Open Shut Them
Traditional Song # 18
added lyrics by Denie Riggs

Open, shut them. Open, shut them.
Let your hands go clap.
Open, shut them. Open, shut them.
Put them in your lap.
Creep them, creep them, Creep them, Creep them.
Right up to your chin.
Open up your little mouth
But do not let them in.
Walk them, walk them, Walk them, walk them
Right down to your toes.
Let them jump up very fast
And hit you on your nose! Ouch!

Blanket Baby*:*
- ♪ *Place your baby on a blanket and do as a massage rhyme.*

Lap Baby:
- ♪ *Place your baby on their back on a blanket. Hold their arms and gently do the appropriate motions with "open" and "shut."*
- ♪ *2nd verse– walk fingers on the tummy up to the chin.*
- ♪ *3rd verse– walk fingers down to the toes and bounce up to the nose.*

Walking Baby:
- ♪ *Position your baby in your lap. Hold your baby's arms and do the appropriate motions.*
- ♪ *2nd verse– walk fingers on the tummy up to the chin.*
- ♪ *3rd verse– walk fingers down to the toes and bounce up to the chin.*

Pat-a-Cake, Pat-a-Cake
Traditional Chant
Pat-a-cake, Pat-a-cake, Baker's man
Bake me a cake as fast as you can.
Roll it, pat it, and mark it with a "B"
And throw it in the oven for baby and me!

Blanket Baby:
♪ *Place your baby on a blanket. Gently take your baby's arms to make the appropriate movement.*

Lap Baby:
♪ *Position your baby in your lap facing you. Gently take hold of your baby's hand to do the appropriate movements.*

> *First two lines, clap hands together.*
> *"Roll it"- move their arms in a circular motion.*
> *"Pat it" – Clap their hands together.*
> *"Mark it with a B" – tickle the baby's tummy*
> *"Throw it" – throw the arms wide apart.*
> *"For baby and me" – clap hands together.*

Walking Baby:
♪ *Use chant as a floor game. Gently slide your baby to your tummy on last line.*

The Little Mice
Traditional Song #19

The little mice go creeping, creeping, creeping.
The little mice go creeping all through the house.

The big black cat goes stalking, stalking, stalking.
The big black cat goes stalking all through the house.

The little mouse goes scampering, scampering, scampering.
The little mouse goes scampering all through the house.

Blanket Baby:
♪ *Use as a massage rhyme on your baby's tummy. 2nd verse goes slower as the cat is stalking. Last verse goes very fast.*

Lap Baby:
♪ *Hold your baby in the burp position or cradle your baby in your arms then move around the room. Verse one is moderate speed, verse two is very slow and verse three is very fast. They will giggle!*

Walking Baby:
♪ *Use as a cat and mouse game,*
   The little mouse (toddler) tip toes around the room.
   The big black cat (parent) takes big steps and stalks the mouse.
   The little mouse takes off, being chased by the cat (parent).

Five Little Kittens

Traditional Chant
Five little kittens, black and white
Sleeping soundly through the night.
Meow, meow, meow, meow. MEOW!
Time to get up now.

Blanket Baby:
♪ *While baby is lying on a blanket, stroke his/her arms, fingers legs or toes. Gently massage each finger beginning with the thumb (or big toe) as you say "meow."*

Lap Baby:
♪ *While baby is lying on a blanket, stroke his/her arms, fingers legs or toes. Gently massage each finger beginning with the thumb (or big toe) as you say "meow." Tickle towards the tummy on the last line.*

Walking Baby:
♪ *Use as a clapping song or a lap bounce. Goose on the last line.*
♪ *Use as a finger play with each finger or toe. Rhythmically chant as you wiggle.*

This Little Piggy Went to Market
Traditional Chant
This little piggy went to market.
This little piggy stayed home.
This little piggy had roast beef.
This little piggy had none.
This little piggy cried...
Wee, wee, wee, wee, wee,
All the way home.

Blanket Baby:
♪ *Place your baby on his/her back on a blanket. Use as a massage rhyme.*

Lap Baby:
♪ *Wiggle each toe starting with the big toe. On "Wee, Wee, Wee," run fingers up the leg to the tummy.*

Walking Baby:
♪ *Use as a lap bounce with your baby facing you. Bounce to the rhythm of the chant. Goose on the last line.*

Whoops Johnny
Traditional Chant

<u>Johnny</u>, Johnny, Johnny, Johnny,
Whoop's Johnny, Whoop's Johnny.
Johnny, Johnny, Johnny.

Substitute your baby's name for <u>Johnny</u>.

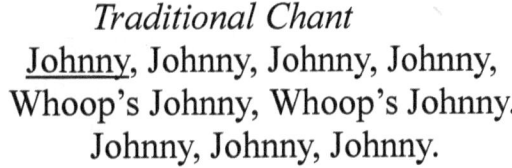

Blanket Baby:
♪ *Place your baby on a blanket. Use as massage rhyme.*
♪ *Tap your baby's feet together in rhythm to the chant.*

Lap Baby:
♪ *While your baby is lying on a blanket, tap each finger starting with the pinkie, until you get to the pointer. Slide down toward the thumb on "Whoops" and hit the thumb on last "Johnny". Repeat as you go back towards the pinkie.*
♪ *Use as a lap bounce.*

Waling Baby:
♪ *Use chant as a floor game, goosing on the "whoops!"*

This Little Cow Eats Grass
Traditional Chant
This little cow eats grass.
This little cow eats hay.
This little cow drinks water.
This little cow runs away.
And this little cow does nothing
But lies down all day.
We'll chase <u>her</u>, and chase her, and chase her
And chase her away.

Substitute: <u>him.</u>

Blanket Baby:
♪ *Place your baby on a blanket. Use as massage rhyme.*
♪ *Tap your baby's feet together in rhythm to the chant.*

Lap Baby:
♪ *While your baby is lying on a blanket, wiggle each toe starting with the big toe. On 'we'll chase her' run your fingers around and around the tummy to goose.*
♪ *Use as a lap bounce with your baby facing you or towards the group.*

Waling Baby:
♪ *Use this chant as a floor game, goosing on the 'chase <u>her</u>!'*

The Family Chant
Traditional Chant
This is the mother,
This is the father,
This is the brother tall.
This is the sister,
This is the baby,
Oh, how we love them all.

Blanket Baby:
♪ *Place your baby on a blanket. Use as massage rhyme.*
♪ *Tap your baby's feet together in rhythm to the chant.*

Lap Baby:
♪ *While your baby is lying on a blanket, wiggle each toe starting with the big toe. On 'how we love them all' goose your baby's tummy.*
♪ *Use as a lap bounce with your baby facing you or towards the group.*

Walking Baby:
♪ *Use this chant as a floor game, goose on the last line.*

Note:
♪ *When using your baby's fingers, begin with the thumb.*

Floor and Chair Games
For Your
Perfect Praise Baby

Older babies spend much of their time on the floor. They love it when you join them.

Blanket Baby:
♪ *Very young babies are not able to do these games as they cannot hold their head up. Use these chants as massage rhymes or gentle lap bounces.*

Lap Baby:
♪ *Lap babies enjoy it when you get on the floor with them. They enjoy these games.*

♪ *Sit in a chair and position your baby facing you or towards the group. Gently lower your baby between your legs on the 'punch' of each chant.*

Walking Baby:
♪ *Lay on the floor on your back with your knees drawn up to your chest. Place your baby on their tummy on your lower legs. Bounce to the rhythm of the chant. On the 'punch,' raise your legs and let your child gently slide down to your tummy.*

The Jack-in-the-Box
Traditional Song #20
The jack-in-the-box jumps up.
The jack-in-the-box goes flop.
The jack-in-the-box goes round and round.
And the lid comes down with a plop!

Blanket Baby:
♪ *Very young babies are not able to do this game as they cannot hold their head up. Use this chant as a massage rhyme or a gentle lap bounce.*

Lap Baby:
♪ *Position your baby in your lap facing you. Bounce to the beat of the rhythm. Gently lower your baby between your legs on 'plop!'*

Walking Baby:
♪ *Lie on your back on the floor. Place your child on their tummy on your lower legs. Bounce to the beat of the chant. Stretch your legs up and let your child slide down onto the your tummy on the 'plop!'*

Little Fire Fighters
Traditional Chant
All the little fire fighters
Sleeping in a row.
Ring goes the bell and…
Down the pole they go.

Blanket Baby:
- ♪ Very young babies are not able to do this game as they cannot hold their head up. Use this chant as a massage rhyme or a gentle lap bounce.
- ♪ Use as a rhythmic chant when changing their diaper, tapping their feet together.

Lap Baby:
- ♪ Position your baby in your lap, facing you. Bounce to the rhythm of the chant. Gently lower your baby towards the floor on last line.

Walking Baby:
- ♪ Lie on your back on the floor. Place your baby on his/her tummy on your lower legs. Bounce to the beat of the chant. Gently shake the child on 'Ring'. Stretch your legs up and let your child slide gently down onto your tummy on the last line.

Our Darling Little Baby
Rhyme by Denie Riggs
©2004
Our darling little baby,
We don't mean maybe
We'll wipe your tears away.
Our darling little baby,
We don't mean maybe
Our love for you will stay.

Blanket Baby:
- ♪ *Very young babies are not able to do this game as they cannot hold their head up. Use this chant as a massage rhyme or a gentle lap bounce.*
- ♪ *Use as massage rhyme when changing your baby's diaper.*
- ♪ *Gently caress your baby's cheek when rocking him/her to sleep.*

Lap Baby:
- ♪ *Position your baby in your lap, facing you. Bounce to the rhythm of the chant. Give a hug on last line.*

Walking Baby:
- ♪ *Lie on your back on the floor. Lay your baby on his/her tummy on your lower legs. Bounce to the beat of the chant. Raise your legs on the last line and let your child slide down to your tummy, giving a hug.*

Humpty Dumpty
Traditional Chant

Humpty Dumpty sat on the wall.
Humpty Dumpty had a great fall.
All the kings horses and all the kings men
Couldn't put Humpty together again.

Blanket Baby:
- ♪ *Very young babies are not able to do this game as they cannot hold their head up. Use this chant as a massage rhyme or a gentle lap bounce.*
- ♪ *When changing a diaper, this chant makes a great foot tapping activity.*

Lap Baby:
- ♪ *Position your baby in your lap facing you. Hold his/her hands. Gently bounce to the rhythm of the chant. On 'great fall' drop your legs and let the baby fall slightly down. On the last line, bring them back up gently.*
- ♪ *Use as a toe wiggle, starting with the big toe. Wiggle one toe on each line until the last and then 'goose' them.*

Walking Baby:
- ♪ ***Sit*** *on the floor with your knees raised in a 90-degree angle. Your child sits on your knees with his/her feet on your tummy. Bounce in rhythm of the chant. On the 'fall', lower your legs to the floor. Slide back up on 'together again.'*

Two Little Apples

Traditional Song #21
Two little apples smiled at me.
Way up high in the apple tree
I shook that tree as hard as I could.
Down came the apples.
MMMM... they were good.

Blanket Baby:
♪ Very young babies are not able to do this game as they cannot hold their head up. Use this chant as a massage rhyme or a gentle lap bounce.

Lap Baby:
♪ Position your baby in your lap facing you. Bounce to the beat of the song. Gently drop the baby down between your legs on 'Down came the apples'. Bring them back up and gently squeeze them on the last line.

Walking Baby:
♪ Lie on your back on the floor with your knees up. Place baby on his/her tummy on your lower legs. Bounce to the rhythm. Gently shake on the third line. Raise your legs to gently let your baby slide down on the fourth line. Kiss your baby on the last line.

Jack & Jill
Traditional Song ◎#22
Jack and Jill went up the hill
To fetch a pail of water.
Jack fell down…. and broke his crown….
And Jill came tumbling after.

Blanket Baby:
♪ *Very young babies are not able to do this game as they cannot hold their head up. Use this chant as a massage rhyme or a gentle lap bounce.*

Lap Baby:
♪ *Position your baby in your lap facing you. Bounce to the beat of the song. Gently drop the baby down between your legs on "Jack fell down". On "broke his crown" return to original position. Goose on 'tumbling after'.*

Walking Baby:
♪ *Lie on your back on the floor with your knees up. Place your child either sitting or laying on your lower legs. Bounce to the rhythm of the song. Raise your legs to permit your baby to gently slide down on the third line. Goose on the last line.*

Bouncing Games
For Your
Perfect Praise Baby

Researchers have determined that bouncing your baby enhances their brain function. Every mom knows that instinctively.

A fun activity for a lap baby is the bouncing swings that hang from a door frame. These are wonderful time savers for you, and enjoyable for the baby also. Turn on their favorite CD nearby and let them *jump to the beat!*

Here are positions to use while bouncing your baby so that babies of all ages may enjoy and be enhanced by this activity.

Blanket Baby:
- ♫ *Hold your newborn or very young baby in the burp position. Walk around the room, bouncing to the beat.*
- ♫ *Use these chants as massage rhymes.*

Lap Baby:
- ♫ *Hold your baby facing you. Bounce them gently to the beat of the song/chant. Do the appropriate movement as indicated by each of the lyrics. The baby will soon remember and anticipate the 'punch'.*
- ♫ *These bouncing activities may also be used as massage rhymes and circle dances.*

Walking Baby:
- ♫ *Older babies will enjoy these games as lap bounces and floor games. Position the baby in your lap facing you. Take hold of his hands and gently bounce to the beat of the chant. Do the appropriate movement as indicated by each of the lyrics. The baby will soon remember and anticipate the 'punch'.*

Note: Each activity in this section gives specific ideas of how to hold your baby. You may try other positions. The important thing is to have fun and be safe. Remember to gently bounce your baby, never overdo.

Walter, Walter Wag Tail

Traditional Song #23
Walter, Walter Wag Tail
Sat upon a pole
He wagged his tail,
And wagged his tail…
'Til he fell down the hole.

Blanket Baby:
- ♪ Use this chant as a massage rhyme or a foot tapping activity while you change the diaper.

Lap Baby:
- ♪ Position your baby in your lap facing you or towards the group. Bounce to the rhythm of the chant.
- ♪ On 'wagged his tail,' swing slightly to the left and right.
- ♪ Let your child fall gently between your legs on 'Til he fell down the hole.'
- ♪ If your child is facing away, gently lower them to the floor by sliding him/her down your legs.

Walking Baby:
- ♪ Lie on your back with your knees up. Place your child on your lower legs. Bounce to the rhythm of the chant. Raise your legs on the last line and allow the child to "fall down the hole" onto your tummy.

Ride a Little Horsy
Traditional Chant
Ride a little horsy
Going down town.
Take care of baby,
Don't you fall down.

Blanket Baby:
♪ *Use this chant as a massage rhyme or a foot tapping activity while you change the diaper.*

Lap Baby:
♪ *Position your baby sitting in your lap facing toward you or towards the group. Bounce gently to the rhythm of the chant. On the last line, gently lower your legs to lower your baby.*

Walking Baby:
♪ *Sit with your legs stretched out on the floor. Place your baby on your lower legs and bounce your child like riding a horse. On the last line, goose your baby.*

The Horse Chant

Traditional Chant
This is the way the ladies ride:
Prim, prim, prim, prim.
This is the way the gentlemen ride:
Trim, trim, trim, trim.
This is the way the hunters ride:
A-gallop, a-gallop, a-gallop, a-gallop.
This is the way the farmer's ride:
Hobblety-hoe, hobblety-hoe,
hobblety, hobblety, hobblety-hoe.
This is the way the astronauts ride…WEE!

Blanket Baby:
♪ *Use this chant as a massage rhyme or a foot tapping activity while you change your baby's diaper.*

Lap Baby:
♪ *Stand, holding your baby in the burp position. Do a bouncing movement with a slight variation for each type of rider. This chant is especially good for a fussy baby.*

Walking Baby:
♪ *Position your baby in your lap facing towards your or towards the group. Bounce to the rhythm.*
- *Ladies ride- bounce light.*
- *Gentlemen ride- low voice and stronger bounce.*
- *Hunters- bounce high and fast (but gently)*
- *Farmers- swing baby from side to side.*
- *Astronauts- raise the baby like a rocket blasting off!*

Riding On A Pony
Traditional Song #24

Riding on a pony, a pony, a pony
Riding on a pony here we go.

Riding on a pony, a pony, a pony
Riding on a pony here we go

Riding on a pony, a pony, a pony
Riding on a pony…

Whoa! (Lean to the right.)
Whoa! (Lean to the left.)
Wee! (Raise the child over your head.)

Blanket Baby:
♪ *Use this chant as a massage rhyme or a foot tapping activity while you change the diaper.*

Lap Baby:
♪ *Stand, holding your baby in the burp position. Bounce to the beat as you walk around the room.*

Walking Baby:
♪ *Position your baby in your lap facing you or toward the group. Bounce to the rhythm of the chant.*

♪ *Bounce with the meter of the music. On 'whoa' lean child far to the right first, then to the left. On last 'Wee', gently lift them high!*

I Know a Little Pony
Traditional Song #25
I know a little pony
Her name is Dapple-Gray
She lives down in the meadow
Not very far away.
She goes nimble, nimble, nimble
And trot, trot, trot.
And then she stops and waits a bit…(pause)
Gallop, gallop, gallop!   Wee!

Blanket Baby:
♪ *Use this chant as a massage rhyme or a foot tapping activity while you change the diaper.*

Lap Baby:
♪ *Stand, holding your baby in the burp position; walk around the room bouncing slightly.*
♪ *This activity greatly calms an agitated baby, especially when you sing along.*

Walking Baby:
♪ *Hold your baby in your lap facing you. Gently hold his/her hands. Bounce to the rhythm of the song. Bounce high on the last three gallops and gently lift your baby high overhead on 'Wee!'*

Mother and Father and Uncle John
Traditional Chant

Mother and Father and Uncle John
Went to town, one by one. (Stop)
Mother fell off. Kink! (Lean child to the right.)
Father fell off. Kink! (Lean child to the left.)
And Uncle John rode on,
and on, and on, and on, and on.

Blanket Baby:
♪ *Use this chant as a massage rhyme or a foot tapping activity while you change the diaper.*

Lap Baby:
♪ *Holding your baby in the burp position, walk around the room bouncing slightly.*
♪ *Holding your baby in a cradle position, gently swing him/her as you walk and bounce to the beat.*

Walking Baby:
♪ *Position your baby in your lap facing toward you or towards the group.*
- *Bounce to the rhythm of the chant*
- *Lean your baby to the right and left as directed by the lyrics.*
- *Get bouncier and faster on the last line.*

♪ *Use as a floor game following the lyrics of the chant.*

See the Pony Galloping
Traditional Song #26

See the pony galloping, galloping
Down the country lane.
See the pony galloping, galloping
Down the country lane.
See the pony coming home all tired out.
See the pony coming home all tired out.

Blanket Baby:
♪ *Use this chant as a massage rhyme or a foot tapping activity while you change the diaper.*

Lap Baby:
♪ *Stand, holding your baby in the burp position. Walk and bounce gently to the rhythm of the chant.*
♪ *Position your child in your lap facing toward you or toward the group. Bounce gently to the rhythm of the chant.*

Walking Baby:
♪ *Use as a floor game. Sit with legs outstretched. Place your baby on your lower legs and bounce your legs. Get slower and slower with the music. Collapse at the end, while keeping the baby secure in your grasp.*

I'm Riding My Horse
Song #27

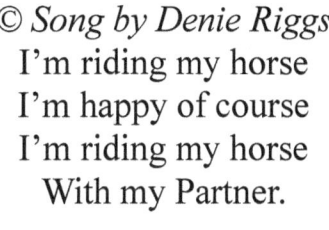

© *Song by Denie Riggs*
I'm riding my horse
I'm happy of course
I'm riding my horse
   With my Partner.

I'm riding my horse
I'm happy of course
I'm riding my horse
   To my music.

I'm riding my horse
I'm happy of course
I'm riding my horse
To see Grandma.
   Whoa! Horsy!

Blanket Baby:
- ♫ *Use this chant as a massage rhyme or a foot tapping activity while you change the diaper.*
- ♫ *Stand, holding your baby in the burp position. Walk and bounce to the rhythm of the song.*
- ♫ *Sit on a chair with your legs crossed. Hold your child on your knee, facing you or facing toward the group. Bounce to the beat. Rare back on Whoa!*

Lap Baby:
- ♫ *Sit on the floor with your legs extended. Place your baby on your lower legs and bounce to the beat. Rare back on Whoa.*
- ♫ *Lie on your back on the floor with your knees bent. Place your baby on his/her tummy on top of your lower legs. Bounce to the rhythm of the song. Let your baby slide down your legs to your tummy on last line.*

Instrumental Games
For Your
Perfect Praise Baby

Songs in this section work well with hand-held rhythm instruments. Lightweight maracas and egg shakers are enjoyed by an older *Perfect Praise Baby*. They also enjoy hand drums. Triangles, sticks and tambourines are too difficult for them to handle.

Blanket Baby:
♪ Very young babies are not able to grasp an egg shaker or a maraca. Use songs in this section for massage rhymes and for general listening enjoyment.

Lap Baby:
♪ Beginning at about five months, your baby will begin to be able to hold and shake the maracas, that is, when they aren't chewing on them!
♪ Around age six months, they may begin to hold other instruments.

Walking Baby:
♪ Walking babies enjoy banging on everything around. Let them... as that is part of their development (and your enjoyment!) Just make sure that their environment is baby-proof!

Everybody Praise the Lord
Song by Denie Riggs 🎵#28

Everybody <u>tap</u> <u>your</u> <u>drums</u>
Together now and praise the Lord.
Everybody tap your drums,
Together now and praise the Lord.
Everybody tap your drums,
Together now and praise the Lord.
Everybody praise the Lord.

Substitute: Everybody <u>tap</u> <u>your</u> <u>tambourine</u> <u>right</u> <u>now</u> …

Twinkle, Twinkle Little Star
Traditional Song 🎵#29

Twinkle, twinkle little star
How I wonder what you are.
Up above the world so high.
Like a diamond in the sky.
Twinkle, twinkle little star
How I wonder what you are.

It's Music Time
Song 🎵#30
© *Song by Denie Riggs*

<u>Shake your eggs</u>, it's music time.
Music time, music time.
Shake your eggs, it's music time.
Let's all sing together.

♪ Shake your <u>bells</u>.
♪ Thump your knees.
♪ Make up other verses.

This Little Light of Mine

Traditional Song #31

This little light of mine
I'm gonna let it shine.
This little light of mine,
I'm gonna let it shine.
Let it shine, let it shine, let it shine.

Wheels on the Bus

Traditional Song #32

The wheels on the bus go 'round and 'round.
'Round and 'round.
'Round and 'round.
The wheels on the bus go 'round and 'round.
All through the town.

2. The horn on the bus goes beep, beep, beep…
3. The friends on the bus go bounce, bounce, bounce…

Make up other verses...
- ♪ The babies on the bus go wah, wah, wah…
- ♪ The daddies on the bus go yak, yak, yak…
- ♪ The mommies on the bus go shh, shh, shh…

Tick Tock
Song ⊙#33
© Song by Denie Riggs

Tick, tock, tick, tock, tick, tock
Goes the clock.
Tick, tock, tick, tock,
Around, around and never stops.
Tick, tock, tick, tock, tick, tock,
Goes the clock.
Tick, tock, tick, tock,
Around, around and 'round.

Hickory, Dickory Dock
Traditional Song ⊙#34
Hickory, Dickory Dock.
The mouse ran up the clock.
The clock struck "ONE"
And down he run...
Hickory, Dickory Dock!

If You're Happy and You Know It
Traditional Song #35

If you're happy and you know it… <u>clap your hands</u>.
If you're happy and you know it…clap your hands.
If you're happy and you know it
Then your face will surely show it.
If you're happy and you know it clap your hands.

♪ Substitute <u>shake your bells.</u>

♪ Substitute <u>thump your knees.</u>

Xylophone Songs
For Your
Perfect Praise Baby

Music researchers have found that the xylophone is an excellent tool to use for ear training and impartation. When the xylophone joins with *solfege* singing, the impartation is incredible. (See '*What to Sing*' in this manual.)

A child's ear is being trained the first five years of their life. However, the younger that you start the better. *Perfect Praise, Inc.* recommends that you use the xylophone daily with your *Perfect Praise Baby*.

It is important that your xylophone be precision-tuned, not just a toy, so that your child's ear training will be imparted accurately.

Solfege and Xylophone Stimulation Exercises

Our *solfege* stimulation exercises are based on the C major scale. The C major scale and its related *solfege* is notated here.

do   re   mi   fa   sol   la   ti   do

To help acquaint you with *solfege* singing, you might want to use a permanent marker to write the *solfege* name on each tone block of your xylophone so it will be in front of you when you sing.

Pronouncing *solfege* syllables:
> *DO* pronounced *dough*
> *RE* pronounced *ray*
> *MI* pronounced *me*
> *FA* pronounced *fah*
> *SOL* pronounced *sole*
> *LA* pronounced *lah*
> *TI* pronounced *tee*

I Know

Words and Music by Denie Riggs  Copyright 1999

I know that ba-by Je-sus. Was born on Christ-mas day. I
Do do do do do do do Re re re re re re. Mi

know His moth-er, Ma-ry Then laid Him in the hay. The
mi mi mi mi mi mi. Fa fa fa fa fa fa Sol

an-gels told the shep-herds Just where this ba-by lay. I
sol sol sol sol sol sol La la la la la la. Ti

know the wise men saw the star and came from far a-way!
ti ti ti ti ti ti ti do do do do do do!

Do ti la sol fa mi re do Sol do!

The Flea

Traditional Chant

Circle Dances
For Your
Perfect Praise Baby

Circle Dances are fun activities to do in a small group or at home in front of your mirror.

Basic Carrying Positions

Blanket Baby:
♪ *Cradle your baby in your arms facing forward.*
♪ *Hold your baby in the burp position... carefully supporting their head.*

Lap Baby Variations:
♪ *Cradle your baby in your arms (facing forward):*
   ♪ *Swing back and forth.*
   ♪ *Sway from side to side.*
   ♪ *Walk in a circle.*
   ♪ *Walk in a circle, changing directions.*
   ♪ *Take four steps in and four steps back.*

Walking Baby:
♪ *Babies love the interaction with other babies for circle games during music class. Hold them facing forward so they may see each other.*
   ♪ *Use instrumental music. Use jazz and instrumental folk music.*
   ♪ *When using classical music, attempt to provide examples from many historical periods, because differing styles of music have different meters and feel. Use upbeat music between 120-136 beats per minute.*

Folk Dance Steps

Listening to your favorite song, do the following movements:

Step bounce, step bounce, step bounce, step bounce,
Walk, two, three, four, five, six, seven, eight.
Step bounce, step bounce, step bounce, step bounce,
Walk, two, three, four, five, six, seven, eight.
IN two, three, four.
OUT two, three, four.
Slow turn, three, four, five, six, seven, eight.
IN two, three, four.
OUT two, three, four.
Slow turn, three, four, five, six, seven, eight.

Bingo

Traditional Song ⊘#36

There was a farmer, had a dog and Bingo was his name-o.
B-I-N-G-O, B-I-N-G-O, B-I-N-G-O and Bingo was his name-o.
B-I-N-G-O

♪ *Hold your baby as appropriate for his/her age.*
♪ *Follow **Folk Dance Steps** above except do only one slow turn at the end.*

Make a Joyful Noise
Song #37
© Song by Denie Riggs

Make a joyful noise, rejoice.
Make a joyful noise, rejoice.
Make a joyful noise, rejoice.
Make a joyful noise, rejoice.

For Jesus Christ is risen,
Let's crown Him King of Kings!
Worship and bow before His throne.
For Jesus Christ is risen,
Let's crown Him King of Kings
Worship, and make a joyful noise.

A Circle Worship Dance:
- ♫ *Hold your baby as required by your baby's development.*
- ♫ *Follow **Folk Dance Steps** except do only one slow turn at the end.*

Clap Your Hands

Traditional Song ♫*#38*

Clap, clap, clap your hands
Clap your hands together.
Clap, clap, clap your hands
Clap your hands together.

'Round and 'round and 'round we go
'Round and 'round and 'round.
'Round and 'round and 'round we go
'Round and 'round and 'round.

Blanket Baby:
♪ *Hold your baby in burp position or facing forward. Gently bounce to the beat.*

Lap Baby:
♪ *Carry your baby and bounce to the beat. Circle to the right on chorus.*

Walking Baby:
♪ *Your walking baby may enjoy toddling about on the chorus. Take their hand and guide them.*

Hoop Song
Traditional Song #39
'Round and around and around we go
Not too fast, not too slow.
'Round and around and around we go
'Round and around and around.

Blanket Baby:
♪ *Use as a massage rhyme after bath.*

Lap Baby:
♪ In class: Hold your baby facing forward. Let the baby hold the hoop and circle slowly with the group.
♪ At home: Hold your child facing forward and move around the living room.

Walking Baby:
♪ At home: A walking baby will enjoy holding hands with you to walk around the room.
♪ In class: Let your child hold on to the hula hoop and walk around with you holding their other hand.

Looby Loo

Traditional *Song* 🎵#40

Here we go Looby Loo
Here we go Looby Light.
Here we go Looby Loo
All on a Saturday night.

You put your <u>right side</u> in
You put your <u>right side</u> out.
You give your side a shake, shake, shake
And turn yourself about.

Here we go Looby Loo
Here we go Looby Light.
Here we go Looby Loo
All on a Saturday night.

♪ *Hold your baby facing forward. On the first stanza, take four steps in, then four steps out. Repeat. On second stanza, do the movements as directed by words.*

♪ *Substitute <u>left side</u>.*

♪ *Substitute <u>whole self</u>.*

Hokey Pokey

Traditional Song 🎵#41
Your put your <u>right side</u> in
You put your right side out,
You put your right side in
And you shake it all about.
You do the Hokey-Pokey,
And you turn yourself around
That's what it's all about.

♪ *Hold your baby facing forward. Bounce to the beat of the music.*

♪ *Substitute: <u>Left side</u>.*

♪ *Substitute: <u>Whole self</u>.*

Crab Walk

Song #42
© Song by Denie Riggs

Doing the crab walk.
Doing the crab walk.
Doing the crab walk.
 What do you say?
Doing the crab walk.
Doing the crab walk.
Doing the crab walk.
 All of the day.

Step, slide, step, slide. 1,2,3.
Step, slide, step, slide. Follow me!
Step, slide, step, slide. Watch me go!
Step, slide, step, slide. Jump in a hole!

(Repeat from beginning. At end of verse…'Jump in a hole!')

Blanket Baby:
♪ *Use a massage rhyme or a foot tapping game.*

Lap Baby:
♪ *Hold your baby facing forward. Bounce to feel the beat. Step to the words. Jump forward on 'Jump in a hole!'*

Walking Baby:
♪ *In class: Children and adults form a circle holding hands with your child. Take baby steps during the verse. Pick up and swing your baby into the center of the circle on 'Jump in a hole!'*
♪ *At home: Hold hands with your child and follow the lyrics. Pick your child up and 'jump in a hole!' when appropriate.*

Note: We recommend that you do not pick up your baby by the arms. Instead lift him/her under the arms, pick up and gently swing them in.

Hello/ Goodbye Song
Song ♫#43
© Song by Denie Riggs
Hello, hello, hello.
It's time to say hello.
We'll sing our music…
Put on a show.
Hello, hello, hello.

Goodbye, goodbye, goodbye.
It's time to say goodbye.
We sang our music…
It's time to fly.
Goodbye, goodbye, goodbye.

***

Our
Perfect Praise Baby
Resources

The information contained in our Perfect Praise Baby Book has come from many sources and also compiled throughout many years of teaching. We are not able to remember all of the sources to compile them on paper for you, however these resources were from the main part of our research.

1. Webster's New World College Dictionary, copyright 2002 bt Wiley Publishing, Inc. 850 Euclid Avenue, Cleveland OH 44114. Michael Agnes, Editor
2. Webster's New World College Dictionary, copyright 2002 bt Wiley Publishing, Inc. 850 Euclid Avenue, Cleveland OH 44114. Michael Agnes, Editor
3. Hughes, Ray, The Minstrel Tape Series, 2000 Edition, P.O. Box 440, Wilkesboro, N.C. 28697
4. Hughes, Ray, The Minstrel Tape Series, 2000 Edition, P.O. Box 440, Wilkesboro, N.C. 28697
5. Hughes, Ray, The Minstrel Tape Series, 2000 Edition, P.O. Box 440, Wilkesboro, N.C. 28697
6. Campbell, Don A. *The Mozart Effect*- Avon Books, N.Y. 1997. p 65-78
7. Campbell, Don A. *The Mozart Effect*- Avon Books, N.Y. 1997. p 65-78
8. Campbell, Don A. *The Mozart Effect*- Avon Books, N.Y. 1997. p 66.
9. Article: *Prelude*, Center for Prenatal and Perinatal Music, www.prenatal_music.com/prelude.htm.
10. Campbell, Don A. *The Mozart Effect*- Avon Books, N.Y. 1997. p 67.
11. Gottlieb, Bill,; "Sound Therapy," *New Choices in Natural Healing* (Emmaus, Pa.: Rodale Press 1995) p. 126-127. Also Clair V. Wilson and Leona S. Aiken, "The Effect of Intensity Levels upon Physiological and Subjective Affective Response to Rock Music," *Journal of Music Therapy* 14 (1977): 60-77.
12. Campbell, Don A. *The Mozart Effect*- Avon Books, N.Y. 1997. p 67.
13. Verny, Thomas, MD and Kelly, John. (1981) *The Secret Life of the Unborn Child,* New York, p. 39. Also Hepper, Peter G. and Shahidullah, Sara B., "Development of Fetal Hearing," *Archives of Disease in Children* 71 (1994): 81-87.
14. Gottlieb, Bill, "Sound Therapy," *New Choices in Natural Healing",* (Emmaus, Pa.: Rodale Press 1995) page 127. And Thaut, Michael; Schleiffers, Sandra; and Davis, William, "Analysis of EMG Activity in Biceps and Triceps Muscle in an Upper Extremity Gross Motor Task under the Influence of Auditory Rhythm, *Journal of Music Therapy,* 28 (1991): 64-88.
15. Gottlieb, Bill, "Sound Therapy," *New Choices in Natural Healing",* (Emmaus, Pa.: Rodale Press 1995) page 127. Also Michael Thaut, Sandra Schlieffers and William

Davis, "Analysis of EMG Activity in Biceps and Triceps Muscles in an Upper Extremity Gross Motor Task under the Influence of Auditory Rhythm, " *Journal of Music Therapy,* 28 (1991): 64-88. Also Kate Greller, "Musical Components and Styles Preferred By Young Adults for Aerobic Fitness," *Journal of Music Therapy* 25 (1988): 28-43.

16. Skille, Olav, "Vibro-acoustic Research" 1980-1991, *Music Medicine,* ed. Ralph Spintge and R. Droh (Saint Louis: MMB Music, 1991), p 249.
17. Campbell, Don A. *The Mozart Effect-* Avon Books, N.Y. 1997. p 69.
18. Campbell, Don A. *The Mozart Effect-* Avon Books, N.Y. 1997. p 72-73
19. Campbell, Don A. *The Mozart Effect-* Avon Books, N.Y. 1997.
20. Addiction Research Center: "Music/Endorphin Link," *Brain/Mind Bulletin* (21 January and 11 February 1985): 1-3.
21. Gerace, Buddha, "So, You'd Like to Sing," *Macrobiotics Today* 35 (May/June 1995); 21-22.
22. Bartlett, Dale; Kaufman, Donald; and Smeltekop, Roger. "The Effects of Music Listening and Perceived Sensory Experiences on the Immune System as Measured by Interleukin-1 and Cortisol," *Journal of Music Therapy* 30 (1993): 194-209.
23. Bartlett, Dale; Kaufman, Donald; and Smeltekop, Roger. "The Effects of Music Listening and Perceived Sensory Experiences on the Immune System as Measured by Interleukin-1 and Cortisol," *Journal of Music Therapy* 30 (1993): 194-209.
24. Gilman, S.C., "Beta-Endorphin Enhances Lymphocyte Proliferate Response," *Proceedings of the National Academy of Sciences* 79 (July 1982), 4226-4230.
25. Ralph Spintge, "Music as a Physiotherapeutic and Emotional Means in Medicine," *Musik, Tanz Und Kunst Therapie* (2 March 1988): 79.
26. Campbell, Don A. *The Mozart Effect-* Avon Books, N.Y. 1997. p 71.
27. Ralph Spintge and R Droh, Anxiety, Pain and Music in Anesthesia, *Journal of American Medical Association* (1996) (Basel: Roche Editions, 1983).
28. John Tesh, radio - research study performed at Case Western Reserve University. johntesh.com. Fall 2004
29. Don G. Campbell, The Mozart Effect," Avon Books, N.Y. 1997. p 76. Also: Campbell, Don, G. ed., *Music--Physician for Times to Come*) Wheaton, Ill.: Quest Books, 1991), p. 246.
30. Verny, Dr. Thomas, M.D., with Weintraub, Pamela., *"Tomorrow's Baby, The art and science of parenting from conception through infancy."* Simon and Schuster, New York, NY, 2002, p 98-99.
31. S.K. Collins and K. Kuch, "Music Therapy In the Neonatal Intensive Care Unit," *Neonatal Network* 9 (6): 23-26 (1997).
32. Campbell, Don A. *The Mozart Effect-* Avon Books, N.Y. 1997. p 74-75.
33. Shetler, D.J., "The Inquiry into Prenatal Music Experience; A Report of the Eastman Project." *Pre-and Perinatal Psychology Journal* 3 (3): 171-189 (1980-1987).
34. Verny, Dr. Thomas, M.D., with Weintraub, Pamela., *"Tomorrow's Baby, The art and science of parenting from conception through infancy."* Simon and Schuster, New York, NY, 2002, p 7-11. Also Campbell, Don A., *The Mozart Effect-* Avon Books, N.Y. 1997. p 23-26.
35. Verny, Thomas, MD and Kelly, John. (1981) *The Secret Life of the Unborn Child,*

New York, p. 21.

36. Rauscher, F.H., "Improved Maze Learning Through Early Music Exposure in Rats," *Neurological Research* 20 (1998) 427-432.
37. George Lozanov, Suggestology and Outlines of Suggestology (New York: E.P. Dutton, 1978); Sheila Ostrander and Lynn Schroeder with Nancy Ostrander, *Superlearning 2000* (New York, Delacorte Press, 1994); Also The Lozanov Report, Chris Brewer and Don G. Campbell, *Rhythms of Learning* (Tucson: Zephyr Press, 1991), pp 291-305.
38. Olsho, 1984; Trehub, Bull, and Thorpe, 1984. Also *Musicality from Birth to Five*, Hodges, Donald A., Institute for Music Research, San Antonio, TX.
39. Rauscher, F.H., "Listening To Mozart enhances spatial-temporal reasoning towards neurophysical basis," *Neuroscience Letter* 185 (1): 44-47 (1995).
40. Ballam, Michael, Cassette Tape: Music and the Mind, Doctorate in music from Indiana University. Distributed by IBLP, Box One, Oak Brook, Illinois, U.S.A.
41. Rauscher, F.H., "Music training causes long-term enhancement of preschool children's spatial-temporal reasoning," *Neurological Research* 19 (I): 218 (1997)
42. Ballam, Michael, Cassette Tape: Music and the Mind, Doctorate in music from Indiana University. Distributed by IBLP, Box One, Oak Brook, Illinois, U.S.A.
43. Discover TV Documentary
44. Shuter-Dyson & Gavriel, 1981; Moog, 1976; Also Association for *Pre- and Peri -Natal Psychology and Health*, (Internet: article.) Chamberlain, David; Early and Very Early Parenting, www.birthpsychology.com. Also Article: Stepien, Jeff, Development of Musical Ability from Birth to Childhood, MuSICA Research Notes, (Music and Science Information Computer Archive.) 2000. www.musica.eci.edu. Dr. Norman M. Weinburger, Edit
45. Association for *Pre- and Peri -Natal Psychology and Health*, (Internet: article.) Chamberlain, David; Early and Very Early Parenting, www.birthpsychology.com. Also Article: Stepien, Jeff, Development of Musical Ability from Birth to Childhood, MuSICA Research Notes, (Music and Science Information Computer Archive.) 2000. www.musica.eci.edu. Dr. Norman M. Weinburger, Editor
46. See documentation on file at Perfect Praise, Inc.
47. (Internet) Article. Chamberlain, David; Early and Very Early Parenting, www.birthpsychology.com. Member: Association for *Pre- and Peri -Natal Psychology and Health*, Also, Lafuente, M.j., Grifoll, R., Segerra, J., Soriano, J., Gorba, M.A., and Montesinos, A. (1997). (On-line). *Pre-and Peri-Natal Psychology Journal*, 11, (3), 151-162. Abstract from: Ovid Technologies File: PsychInfo Item: 1997-20104-002. MENC *The National Association for Music Education.*
48. Pediatric neurobiologist Dr. Harry Chugani, Wayne State University.
49. Article: *The Importance of Prenatal Sound and Music*, Column Editor: Giselle E. Whitwell, R.M.T., www.birthpsychology.com/lifebefore/sound1/html
50. Fabien, Maman Dr., the Science of Sound in Healing; *The Role of Music in the Twenty-first Century*. www.healingcancernaturally.com, www.aliceviolet.com/fabien.htm
51. Student documentation on file at Perfect Praise, Inc.
52. Campbell, Don A. *The Mozart Effect-* Avon Books, N.Y. 1997. p 23.
53. Campbell, Don A. *The Mozart Effect-* Avon Books, N.Y. 1997. p 22.
54. Student documentation on file at Perfect Praise, Inc.

55. Meditation Classical Relaxation Volumes, LaserLight, 1991 Delta Entertainment Inc. Los Angeles CA. 90064.
56. Student documentation on file at Perfect Praise, Inc.
57. Trainor, Ms. Laurel, Department of Psychology, Neuroscience and Behaviour, McMaster University, 2005.

Our Own *Perfect Praise Baby* Success Stories

Here is a sampling of case studies from our *Early Childhood Music*® curriculum and schools.

♪ Aware of the Mozart Effect, Abby's mom played classical music to her unborn child through headphones on her tummy. After birth, Abby's environment was filled with music and musical activities. At 16 months of age, Abby had a vocabulary of over 800 words. A coincidence? *No way!*

♪ Susie enrolled in our *Perfect Praise Baby Class* when she was ten months old. Susie's mom knew of the benefits of music from her college days. Susie's dad, being typical, was somewhat skeptical about enrolling their baby in music lessons, but was willing to go along with his wife's desires. However, he immediately began to see the weekly changes in her development. He was excited!

Now, at 29 months old, Susie's developmental skills far surpass her young age. She has advanced fine motor skills normally not found in children under three years old. Her cognitive skills are sharp; she is able to perform simple memorization tasks and has a very large vocabulary. Susie's success is due to the fact that her parents know the value of music. She has been taking music lessons since her early babyhood, and rarely misses a class because music is a priority to this family. As a 2½ year-old, Susie was recently promoted into the three and four year-old music class. Her progress is amazing! A coincidence? *No way!*

♪ Jake's parents enrolled him in a *Perfect Praise Baby Class* when he was nine months old. At that time, Jake scored twelve months on his pediatric developmental chart. Three months later he had progressed significantly to a score of 19½ months. *He progressed 6½ months in development after only three months of lessons.* His *pediatrician* attributed Jake's progress to music class. Jake loves his music class. A coincidence? *No way!*

Our
Give Them the Best Start
Prenatal Curriculum

Your baby's ears begin to form the third week after conception. Sounds, songs, voices and your heartbeat begin to stimulate neural connections in your baby's brain. *Perfect Praise Inc.* has a program for babies *before* they are born called **Give Them the Best Start.**

Scientific research shows us that everything that stimulates an expectant mom, affects her baby. *Give Them the Best Start'* curriculum gives expectant parents vitally important information in regards to music stimulation in your baby <u>*before*</u> birth.

You will learn:
- ♪ Why familiar sounds and familiar music provide comfort and reassurance to your baby.
- ♪ What you can do while expecting to enhance your child's development mentally, socially, and spiritually.
- ♪ The benefits of listening to music while expecting.
- ♪ Our prayer journal gives you daily tools to impart to your baby. It is life changing!

Our full GTBS curriculum consists of:
1. *Give Them the Best Start Manual*
2. *Activity CD*
3. *Classical Praise CD*
4. *Charting Your Baby's Destiny Prayer Journal*
5. *Precision-Tuned Xylophone*

Get complete information on-line at: <u>www.prenatalmusic.net.</u>

We hope that you have enjoyed our
Perfect Praise Baby curriculum.

Perfect Praise Baby

curriculum
makes a great study for a small group,
Sunday School Class
and many other uses and opportunities.

A leader's guide is available.

You can continue to enhance your baby with our
Perfect Praise, Inc
age-specific materials to age eight years and beyond.

Contact us for more information

Perfect Praise, Inc.
P.O. Box 18008
Huntsville, AL 35804